Nurture Faith
Five Minute Meditations
to Strengthen Your Walk with Christ

W. Douglas Hood, Jr.

Foreword by
William J. Carl III, PhD

Parson's Porch Books
www.parsonsporchbooks.com

Nurture Faith: Five Minute Meditations to Strengthen Your Walk with Christ

ISBN: Softcover 978-1-949888-14-0
Copyright © 2018 by W. Douglas Hood, Jr.

All rights reserved. No part of this book may be reproduced or transmitted in any form or by any means, electronic or mechanical, including photocopying, recording, or by any information storage and retrieval system, without permission in writing from the publisher.

Unless otherwise indicated, Scripture quotations taken from the Common English Bible (CEB). Copyright © 2011. Used by permission. All rights reserved.

Nurture Faith

Contents

Foreword	ix
What Leaders Are Saying	xi
Preface	xiii
A Special Word	xiv
Appreciation	xv
The Struggle to Believe	1
A Faith That Gets Noticed by God	2
Knowing God's Will	4
Speaking Wisely	6
Becoming Anxious for God	8
Who Needs God?	10
Plants of Steel	12
Contemplating Heaven	14
Adequate Faith	16
Authentic Faith	17
Discerning Right from Wrong	19
Misreading the Bible	21
Looking Back, Looking Forward	23
The Allure of a Defeated Life	25
Treasure in Clay Pots	27
When Faith Is Difficult	29
Victory on Our Knees	31
The Puzzle of Prayer	33
The Full Development of Faith	35
The Silent Word	37
Something Familiar	39
God's Desire	41
Why?	43
When Our Hearts Are Anxious	45
Uniola paniculata (Sea Oats)	47
Flags on the Beach	49
Sandcastles	51
Beachcombing	53
Sea Glass	55
Pelicans	57
Hope for a Splintered Church	59

Uneasy Worship	61
Knowing God's Will	63
When It Is Difficult to Love Yourself	65
Holy Speech	67
Paying Attention to God	68
Confidence in Christ	70
The Common Life Lived Uncommonly	72
The Scramble for Success	74
More of God	76
Ministry of Imagination	78
The Secret of Spiritual Power	80
Overcommitted Lives	82
Motivated by a Vision	84
Our Compulsion to Complain	86
Willful Submission	88
Living with Tension	90
Our Daily Work	92
When Our Spiritual Energies Fail	94
The Cost of Complaining	96
Fear at Christmas	98
On the Road	100
Distinctive Claims of the Christian Faith	102
God Will Guide Us	104
A Fresh Approach to Prayer	106
Our Responsibility to One Another	108
Living Positively with Our Handicaps	110
Jesus in the Everyday	112
A Sturdy Faith	114
Feeling. Understanding. Believing.	116
Why Go to Church?	118
Eyes of Faith	120
Overcoming Defeat	122
Filled by Christ	124
Faith in Prayer	126
Our Sacred Work	128
Authentic Friendships	130
Complete in Christ	132
Christianity and Communism	134

Doubt and Faith	136
Isn't It Enough to Be Decent?	138
The Responsible Exercise of Faith	140
Life's Disappointments	142
Is Belief in A Personal God Possible?	144
Andrew: The First Disciple	146
Sharing Our Faith Story	148
When Christ Knocks	150
Experiencing A Real and Vivid Faith	152
Disagreements in the Church	154
Remember	156
For This Moment	158
Disillusionment with God	159
Recovering the Adventure of Faith	161
More from Jesus	163
The Ultimate Source of Greatness	165
Where to Begin	167
Loving God with Our Minds	169
The Weight of Guilt	171
An Indecisive Faith	173
Overwhelmed?	175
The Power of Purpose	177
Christmas Confidence	179
When We Are Desperate	181
What Are We to Do with Our Fears?	183
A Faith that Is Good and Pleasing	185
When We Need Help	187
When the Door Remains Closed	189
I Don't Remember Me (Before You)	191
Don't Complain!	193
Living with Tension	195
Dear Hate	197
The Trouble with Pessimists	199
How to Know God Better	201
The Missing Factor in Our Faith	203
Getting Started with Jesus	205
Space Cowboy	207
God's Purpose. God's Call. God's Power	209

When God Seems Distant	211
Unnamed Saints	213
Figuring Out God's Will	215
Happy People	217
Dear God	219
Hesitant Believers	221
What Is Good	223
Taking Jesus Seriously	225
A Prescription for Living	227
I Woke Up in Nashville	229
No Place Available	231
If I Told You	233
The School of Christ	235
There's A Girl	237
Sabal Palmetto	239
The Long Way	241
What God Does for Us	243
(*Location: Via Dolorosa*)	243
Better Man	245
About the Author	247

Foreword

What a wonderful book this is! A great resource for clergy and laity alike. Although some ministers stop reading once they graduate from seminary or divinity school, Doug Hood is clearly not one of them. His bibliography and footnotes alone provide a rich feast from some of the greatest spiritual minds of our age.

This book is creative, thoughtful, inspirational and uplifting all at the same time. Written with a kind of C.S. Lewis/Buechnerian style, one is engaged immediately and drawn in to a way of thinking about one's spiritual life that is both challenging and transformative.

As a theological educator who has now returned to the parish in the summer of 2015, I am particularly interested in ideas shared here that prime the homiletical pump and get the preaching juices flowing. There are many of them!

Lay people who want to think theologically about how to live the Christian life in a multicultural world where there are more Muslims than there are Presbyterians in this country, will find insights in this book into being responsible Christians in a Post-Christendom, twenty-first century world.

As readers plumb the depths of Doug Hood's reflections, exploring these nuggets of biblical and spiritual discernment I predict that they will come away feeling less fearful, more hopeful, less self-centered, more holy, less anxious, more at peace, and ready to take on whatever life throws at them because they will know that with God they are never alone. God is right there by our side whispering in our ears words of encouragement and challenge.

The personal reflections in this wonderful book resonate with all of us because the very issues Doug admits he's wrestled with throughout his life are often the same ones we've face ourselves. Thus the line he no doubt hears frequently after worship on Sundays, "Preacher, you were speaking directly to me today!"

~ **William J. Carl III, PhD** ~ Senior Pastor, Independent Presbyterian Church, Birmingham, Alabama, Former President, Pittsburgh Theological Seminary

What Leaders Are Saying

In his helpful devotional guide, *Nurture Faith: Five Minute Meditations to Strengthen Your Walk with Christ*, Doug Hood invites us to join him in the spiritual disciplines that have made him an exemplary pastor, preacher, husband and father. If we will assimilate the spiritual disciplines of scripture, meditation, and prayer into our daily routine, we will grow in our faith in Jesus Christ. But watch out…these devotionals might just change your life…as they are changing mine!"
(Rev. Dr. Thomas K. Tewell, Former Executive Director, Macedonian Ministry)

Nurture Faith: Five Minute Meditations to Strengthen Your Walk with Christ by Doug Hood provides a meaningful resource for people of faith as it blends Biblical passages with experiences of today, resulting in a meditation guide as well as a self-help manual. By consistently relating God's word with current examples, Dr. Hood has revealed his own struggles in being faithful while providing insight into possible responses to temptations and challenges which impact all Christians in one way or another on their faith journey.
(Heath Rada, Moderator, 2014 General Assembly Presbyterian Church USA.)

For those who want accessible, practical, and challenging wisdom to grow in faith and understanding of the Christian life, I can think of no better daily diet than Pastor Hood's devotionals. One hundred percent organic--distilled from years of faithful service in the trenches of real life.
(Bruce Main, President/Founder, UrbanPromise Ministries)

Fear, anxiety, doubt, brokenness, discouragement and desperation; courage, confidence and hope - these are emotions each of us experience; emotions of the heart and soul. Here, in these meditations, Doug Hood addresses each experience in a simple, direct and comforting manner, with scripture as his foundation and a brief prayer to close. I am grateful for this collection of meditations which nurture my faith each day. Gathered here are reflections for the faithful and for those who seek more from their walk with Christ.
(John Randolph, Attorney, West Palm Beach, Florida)

Here is a word for everyone seeking encouragement, but particularly helpful for those inside the church – pastors, educators, lay leaders, members. In brief meditations, Doug Hood artfully connects God's Word to our daily experiences. Insightful, articulate and inspirational, Dr. Hood's pastor's heart and active personal faith shine through brightly.
(Daniel W. Klein, Irving, Texas, Retired President, Texas Presbyterian Foundation, and now a Church Consultant)

With countless options for devotionals in bookstores, it can be a challenge to pick out the ones that are theologically sound, relevant and fresh. I have found that wonderful mix in Nurture Faith: Five Minute Meditations to Strengthen Your Walk with Christ. In every meditation, Dr. Hood offers timely and honest insight to the words of Scripture and offers encouragement for followers of Christ. This book is filled with inspiring words of faith and grace for small group studies, in church committee meetings, and for individual devotional time.
(Catherine Cavazos Renken, Pastor, Kirkwood Presbyterian Church, Kennesaw, Georgia)

Preface

God urgently wants you to claim the purpose for your life. Living into this unique purpose powerfully transforms the ordinary into the extraordinary. Not only will life be purposeful – you will encounter a new depth of meaning and joy as well.

The brief meditations in this book do not answer questions about the point of your life. Rather, they provide reflections upon God's Word that grows confidence in God's powerful ability to direct you to identify and claim what you were created to do; meditations that encourage the heart and refresh the soul. The intention is that you read one each morning at the start of your day. If you are in a relationship with someone, I encourage you to share the reading together.

In a passionate spiritual autobiography, *Girl Meets God: On the Path to a Spiritual Life*, Lauren F. Winner shares that she was raised the child of a Jewish father and a lapsed Southern Baptism mother. The moment came, as it does for all of us, that Winner had to make a faith decision for her own life. She chooses to become an Orthodox Jew. Yet, following her faith decision, Winner experiences what she describes as an inescapable courtship by "a very determined carpenter from Nazareth." She eventually converts to the Christian faith.

My hope is that in these pages you will encounter that "very determined carpenter from Nazareth." Root each day in God's Word before you encounter the words of anyone else. By this regular practice you will find certainty and direction in your journey of faith. Seek God's purposes for your life and be prepared for the extraordinary!

W. Douglas Hood, Jr.

A Special Word

Ecclesiastes teaches that there's nothing new under the sun. "People may say about something: 'Look at this! It's new!' But it was already around for ages before us." Ecclesiastes 1:10 (Common English Bible) My own devotional life has been nourished by the work of many, particularly Henry Sloane Coffin, J.H. Jowett, Robert J. McCracken, David H.C. Read, Bryant M. Kirkland, Barbara Brown Taylor, Thomas Long, and Thomas K. Tewell. Their "fingerprints" are scattered throughout this collection, and for that I am grateful.

Appreciation

The membership of the First Presbyterian Church of Delray Beach, Florida, who has welcomed my ministry for six years as their pastor. Together we have sought to nurture faith within our own community of faith as well as in the local community. They have loved my family and me, received my ministry with joy, encouraged me in my own journey of faith, and provided for my family's material needs. They continue to make my ministry among them one of delight.

Nancy Fine is a dear friend and colleague in ministry. Her administrative wisdom and support continue to be a treasure in my ministry. Unquestionably, I am a better pastor because of her.

Paul and Andy Miller, Rob and Joan Tanner, Kenneth and Vandy Janson, Leo and Pat Phillips, Anne Gaudree, Charles and Kathy Gray, and Frank and Becky Wyatt, members of First Presbyterian Church of Delray Beach, whose love, encouragement and support for my family have provided numerous blessings

Skip and Leslie Randolph, cherished friends who have shared vacations with my wife, Grace, and me, prayed with and for me and have provided uncommon encouragement for my ministry.

Most importantly, I deeply appreciate my family, my wife Grace, and children, Nathanael and Rachael, who continue to support and encourage my ministry. Grace, you are a woman who embodies Christ-like character. The Lord's truths, wisdom, and immeasurable love and encouragement always come through you. You, along with two remarkable children, have made our life together a joyful place.

The Struggle to Believe

"I have faith; help my lack of faith!"
Mark 9:24 (Common English Bible)

Many who sincerely want to believe in God find believing to be difficult. Faith rarely comes easily. The only way it does come is when we accept where we are on our faith journey and go on from there. Longing to be someplace else along the journey accomplishes nothing, apart from frustration.

At the beginning of a new year, we cannot say I wish I was fifteen pounds less before beginning a New Year's resolution of a healthier lifestyle. Eating better, exercising more and getting more rest must begin where you are. That is what the unidentified man in this story from Mark's Gospel teaches us; we must begin where we are, "Lord, I believe, help my unbelief." He begins from where he is. Within him is a mixture of belief and unbelief. He owns that when he speaks to Jesus.

Each day we may know a little more of God. We can never know all of God. But instead of being occupied with what we don't know we can say, "help me with my unbelief." The man in our story approaches Jesus with both belief and unbelief. Rather than dwelling upon what he doesn't know - or being troubled by what he doesn't understand - he seeks Jesus' help. There is present enough faith to seek more of Jesus. This is a more helpful approach to faith than those who claim they will not believe until they understand fully.

The Christian faith is not established upon right beliefs, right doctrine, or on how much someone believes. The Christian faith is personal, centered upon the person of Jesus. Here, this man in Mark's story instructs us that often we approach faith incorrectly. Rather than trying to understand all the mystery that is God, this man seeks out the person of Jesus; he seeks a relationship. To concentrate on what you don't understand will destroy whatever faith you have. Accepting God's love in the person of Jesus and making your love for him tangible in each day of life results in a faith that will grow from more to more.

In this new year, Heavenly Father, strengthen the little faith I have and help me to trust in your love when life becomes uncertain. Amen.

A Faith That Gets Noticed by God

"He has told you, human one, what is good and what the Lord requires from you: to do justice, embrace faithful love, and walk humbly with your God."
Micah 6:8 (Common English Bible)

Henry Sloane Coffin observes that walking humbly with God has not been characteristic of modern Christians. Coffin pondered deeply on the question of what it means to be a person of faith. I do not know what he thought about this passage from the prophet Micah, but it seems that the prophet has captured it in a nutshell: God's people do justice, embrace faithful love, and walk humbly with God. Here is a demonstration of faith that gets noticed by God.

Recently, the pope made some observations about unchecked capitalism. As a man of deep faith, he felt that the income inequity in the world represents the failure to do what is just by all of God's people. The political and social debate that followed has been fierce. In fact, the rhetoric has been quite heated, if not mean-spirited. Good points have been made by parties across the political spectrum. So have some rather weak arguments been advanced. The point here is not who is right and who is wrong; not whether the pope is right, or the pope is wrong. What has been clear in this rancorous conversation is the lack of humility. Coffin is right. Once we have an opinion, political or otherwise, humility is no longer invited to the party.

Earlier in this chapter from the prophet Micah, the question turns on how much sacrifice is required to be noticed by God; how much sacrifice it takes to please God. Burnt offerings of year-old calves? Thousands of rams with an equally generous amount of oil? Perhaps the sacrifice of our oldest child? The prophet answers that none of that pleases the Lord. What God desires is behavior that demonstrates justice and kindness embodied in a life that shows deference to God.

The wonderful preacher, William Willimon once was asked a very specific question – a specific response to how Christians must live and vote, and act was sought. With considerable wisdom, Willimon answered that his baptismal burden was to preach the Bible. The one who was asking also had a baptismal burden. Their burden was to seek from God through sincere and earnest prayer what obedience to God's Word looked like in their life. One may agree with the pope about the abuse of capitalism. Another may disagree. All of God's people are called to seek – with humility – God's personal claim upon their life and what that means for walking each day with our Lord.

Forgive us, God, for behavior that ignores the possibility of truth in another. Humble our stubborn spirit that we may walk with you in a manner that brings glory to your Son, Jesus Christ. Amen.

Knowing God's Will

"Don't be conformed to the patterns of this world but be transformed by the renewing of your minds so that you can figure out what God's will is – what is good and pleasing and mature."
Romans 12:2 (Common English Bible)

Recently, my friend Tom Tewell shared with me a basic and helpful approach to seeking God's will – an approach he had learned years earlier from Lloyd J. Ogilvie. The place to begin is a careful reading of the Bible and prayer. Seeking God's will in a particular circumstance, or more generally for one's life, must always begin with some grasp of who God is. What can we know of God and how God has worked through human history from God's Word in the Holy Scriptures? God's desire for today will not contradict God's character as disclosed in the Bible. If God is opposed to adultery in the Bible, for instance, God remains opposed to adultery. Simply, we will never discern that God may be calling us to violate our marriage vows.

The second movement to discerning God's will is by consulting with a few trusted people who have demonstrated, in some way, that they listen carefully for God's direction. These will be people who have been widely noticed by others as "paying attention to God" as they live each day. Share with them what you think God may be calling you to do. Then invite them to place what you think you hear alongside what they know of God and God's activity. Is there consistency? Does what you believe God is saying match up with the God your friends have come to know from years of following Christ? Some Christian leaders refer to this practice as "discernment in community." Bring what you hear to a faithful community, so they can say if it makes sense to them from what they know of God.

Finally, pay attention to the opportunities that present themselves – and those that don't. What some may simply call "circumstances" may be powerful indicators of what God is up to in your life. If you believe God is calling you to missionary work overseas and no doors seem to be opening for that to happen, it is well to rethink if God's will has been properly discerned. On the other hand, if you sense God is calling you to partner with Habitat for Humanity for building homes for the poor, and you have particular skills for building homes, and have discretionary time available in your routine rhythm of life and then hear of a specific need from that organization that you can meet, and feel a burden for those who can't afford a home – well, you see where I am going.

Many ask why finding God's will has to be such a struggle. My own take on that is that God planned it that way. It is in the struggle that we go deeper and deeper in a relationship with God. Think of it this way. A meaningful relationship with a spouse is built by paying close attention to their likes and dislikes over a long period of time. We listen carefully when they speak. We watch what makes them happy and what discourages them. We take notice of their idiosyncrasies. This takes effort, naturally. But it is the effort – over time – that results in a deep and satisfying relationship with another. God wants no less from us.

Father God, today I pray that you will instill in my heart patience to seek your will, clarity of understanding and a passionate desire to obey everything Jesus commanded. Amen.

Speaking Wisely

"Do you love life; do you relish the chance to enjoy good things?
Then you must keep your tongue from evil and keep your lips from speaking lies!"
Psalm 34:12-13 (Common English Bible)

It is a rhetorical question, of course. Who doesn't want to be thoroughly alive, enjoying all the good things that life has to offer, to be lifted above the plane of mere existence? To live a large life, a life of spacious activities and with a grand purpose captures our imaginations. This is a life of abounding energy and possesses a deep awareness of the things that bless – both personally and those around us.

The Psalms offer treasured insight for such a life, insight for embracing a spacious life of blessedness, of extracting the secret flavors and essences of things as we live into each day. Very specifically, we are instructed in the wisdom of many who have traveled before us; we are told to exercise wise government over our tongues. Relationships with one another rise to unimaginable heights as the tongue is disciplined and directed to build, to edify and exalt those who hear us. It is as though life receives its nutriments from careful and blessed speech.

Our speech is too often destructive. Poison-soaked speech first poisons the speaker. "Every word we speak recoils upon the speaker's heart, leaves its influence, either in grace or disfigurement," writes that wonderful preacher, J.H. Jowett.[1] Where the tongue is untrue the heart is afraid of exposure. Life is diminished. One may also argue that such speech is lazy speech. Where there is no exercise of restraint or government of the tongue; it is free to roam at will. Therefore, urges the Psalms, keep your tongue from evil and speaking lies. The tongue that is held in severe restriction, the tongue that only shapes words that are good and encouraging to others results in quiet and fruitful happiness.

Undisciplined tongues seem to flourish today. And the world is the poorer for it. Yet, our own lives may move to a higher plane simply by a personal revolt from the disorderly conduct of tongues. The best way to affect a departure from the guile and venom that flows freely around us is to exercise one's self in active good, of words spoken kindly, with pleasantness and grace. The fragrance of our speech will tickle the hearts of others. It may invite them to share in the same wisdom of the Psalms, an invitation to experience a blessed life, full, safe and abounding in good things.

Grant me the wisdom and strength to govern my tongue, O Lord. Help me to use my speech only to encourage, build and edify all who hear me, that my life and theirs will be blessed. Amen.

---

[1]J.H. Jowett, *Thirsting for the Springs: Twenty-Six Weeknight Meditations* (London: H.R. Allenson, Limited, 1907), 188.

Becoming Anxious for God

"One by one, they all began to make excuses."
Luke 14:18 (Common English Bible)

An anxious eye on the clock and the unending fight with time accurately describes the character and tempo of life today. We are a people always on the move, operating on a tight and crowded schedule. The pace of life seems swifter than that of a previous generation, the pressure harder and responsibilities to be borne heavier than they should be for any one person. The tragic consequence for millions is that little time is given to cultivate the life of the soul – little time left to know and enjoy God.

Luke's story offers caution. In this parable, Jesus speaks of a man who prepared a great feast and sent out invitations to his friends to be his guest. One by one they sent their apologies. The first had bought a farm and felt it prudent to go and look it over. The second closed a deal for five oxen and was off to check on them. The third had recently married – perhaps the strongest excuse but an excuse nonetheless. At that the host directed his servant to go out and bring to the feast the poor, the crippled, blind, and lame. Jesus' point is clear. All three men were engaged in perfectly legitimate activities. Yet, so immersed in them were they that they left room in their lives for nothing else.

Jesus' life was also filled with many legitimate activities. Some may say that Jesus' life was burdened with the needs and hurts of others. But do not fail to notice an important distinction between the life lived by Jesus and the life of the men in the parable. Jesus made time for quiet, for prayer, and for God. Precisely because the demands of life exhausted Jesus he would slip away from the crowds and the bustle to be alone with God. If Jesus realized the sustaining need of regular time with God, how much more do we? Jesus' deepest need to get through each day was spiritual. So is ours.

We are a busy people. Occupied and preoccupied by this and that, and the other thing, those things that matter most are often crowded out. Luke's Gospel makes a plea for the human heart and soul – a plea for perspective and recognition of the supreme values for which

Jesus stood. In an overcrowded life, and the pressure and pace being greater than they should be, Jesus's own life calls us to practice discrimination – to choose wisely what will fill our lives, never neglecting to reserve time for the spiritual. The spiritual should have priority over everything else. Our duty to God comes before all other demands placed upon us. Should we become anxious about what we face this day, let us first be anxious for God.

Slow down my heart and quiet my mind, O Lord, that I may simply enjoy you, if but for a few moments this day. Amen.

Who Needs God?

"But the centurion replied, 'Lord, I don't deserve to have you come under my roof. Just say the word and my servant will be healed.'"
Matthew 8:8 (Common English Bible)

Living without God is not a recent invention. From the beginning of history women and men have heard the whisper, "Who needs God?" It was there in the third chapter of Genesis when Satan – having taken the form of a snake – asked the question of the woman, Eve. The question has disturbed every person since that fateful day in the Garden of Eden. How many of us can honestly confess to a desperate need for God? How real a factor is the thought of God in the common moments of each day?

It is my experience that for many people, God resides in the peripheral rather than occupying a central place in their lives. If our felt need for God becomes only occasional we learn, moment by moment and day by day, to live without God. Eventually, it isn't a big step to live entirely without any thought of God. Many who have moved to this place may reject having someone identifying them as an atheist but, in truth, God is no longer real. David H. C. Read once shared that some people in his New York City congregation have confessed that having missed worship and prayer for extended months, life went on much as usual. The question presses, "Who needs God?"

Perhaps the real question in play is, "What is important to us?" If we decide in our hearts that material success, the acquiring of wealth and comfort, is to be our supreme goal, then God may be irrelevant: we don't need God. Make no mistake; there is nothing at all wrong with success – even financial success. It is a question of what is most important. Do we seek to be caught-up in something bigger than ourselves; to be fully engaged with the purposes of God or do we ultimately live for ourselves? If we are totally dedicated to material success, asserts David H. C. Read, then we don't need God. We have one.

Here in Matthew's Gospel a centurion realizes a need for God. One of his servants is desperately ill and there is nothing that the centurion's wealth, position and power can do for the servant. The centurion realizes that he is without the resources that are required. The centurion approaches Jesus and asks for a word of grace, a word that would do for the servant what the centurion is incapable of doing. When the centurion declares to Jesus, "Lord, I don't deserve to have you come under my roof," it is a declaration that the centurion has been living without God. Now he has awakened to the need that has been there all the time. The centurion needs God. And at that very moment the servant was made well.

Increase my desire for you, O God, that I may treasure what truly brings joy. Amen.

Plants of Steel

"I can endure all these things through the power of the one who gives me strength."
Philippians 4:13 (Common English Bible)

The garden center of Home Depot features a selection of plants ideal for home or office called, "Plants of Steel." They are plants that seem to thrive in apparent adversity. Where other plants would wilt for lack of water and sunshine these plants enjoy optimal vitality from neglect. I have purchased several of these plants and it is fascinating to watch them flourish in spite of – or because of – my inattention to their care. They seem to have a preference for hardship.

These plants offer an encouragement for the spiritual life. Difficult circumstances, though never sought, can provide growth. Such growth is clear in the lived experience of the apostle Paul. In this letter to the Church of Philippi, Paul is in captivity at Rome. His supreme mission of preaching the Gospel of Christ appears to be at an end. No longer does Paul have the stimulus of travel, the joy of enriching itineraries or the delight of preaching the good news over the broad landscape of Asia and Greece. That open road has been narrowed to the walls of a prison cell. Yet, there is an absence of gloom in Paul's writing. Throughout this letter of Philippians there is present an incomparable strength and beauty.

Paul's imprisonment does not usher in a season of gloom. Rather, what Paul experiences is a time of spiritual graces. He writes of losing everything for Christ only to realize that what he lost has no value compared to what he has gained in a relationship with Jesus. Within prison walls Paul realizes the broad range and wealth of his spiritual inheritance. While some of his friends referred to his misery, Paul writes of his joy. Though some regretted his poverty, Paul boasts of possessing all that he needs. What appears to be a season of winter for Paul is transformed to an opportunity to be clothed in a fleece robe of strength and hopefulness.

Some today become very poor in difficulty and adversity. When in the natural rhythm of life, they reach desert places or what may feel as an endless winter of the soul, they live without any cheer. Sourness and fretfulness encompass them as the prison walls surrounded Paul.

All of life becomes a menagerie of unpleasant things. Worse, they feel left alone. Paul's incredible witness is that this doesn't have to be their story. Paul writes letters from prison not to share his misery with a sympathetic ear. He writes to invest in others. Investments in other people, in the ministry of our Lord, scatter the gloom, brighten the place of our dwelling and preserve the leaf of our soul from withering. We become plants of steel! More, we will know such joy that the desert of the soul shall rejoice and blossom like a rose.

In the winter of the soul, help me to seek the face of Jesus, to invest in others and experience uncommon strength and joy. In the certain name of my Lord, Jesus Christ, I pray. Amen.

Contemplating Heaven

"Then, we who are living and still around will be taken up together with them in the clouds to meet with the Lord in the air. That way we will always be with the Lord."
I Thessalonians 4:17 (Common English Bible)

Many in the church today occupy their minds and energy with the condition of those who have meager resources. In our community – as in most communities – are the hungry, the addicted and homeless. The common streets of the community which are a blessing to some are unkind to others. Particularly in communities where abundance is easily visible, scarcity is deeply experienced by some. Into this condition of impoverishment are good people who seek to concentrate all their energy in bettering the life that is. The church is at its best because of these people; the Kingdom of God draws a little nearer to earth for their labor of love.

Yet, for all their empathy for the poor, the ceaseless effort to lift the burden for those who suffer there is a larger lesson that is occasionally missed – the value of dwelling upon that place in which we will spend eternity with our Lord. Glimpses of the life to come, stirring the imagination with thoughts of continual communion with our Lord has the capacity to nourish the effort in realizing here on earth that the life that is to be in heaven. And I have discovered that no one works more eagerly than those who, for now and again, permit their thoughts to view the New Jerusalem, the City of God as spoken of in the last book of the Bible, the Book of Revelation.

In these few sentences from I Thessalonians, the Apostle Paul is directing our gaze to something he has seen. Paul's faith is one that has received its nourishment from the steady attention to God and God's present activity in the world. Our own eyes can never hope to see what Paul sees without the same attention to God. As with any relationship, spiritual growth demands intentionally spending time with the one we hope to spend eternity. Naturally, that requires the regular reading and contemplation of God's Word in the Bible.

It is good to occasionally think about the place to which we are all moving toward. Such a steady, frequent and regular contemplation of life with God gives fresh energy for the practical life of faith. The door between our heart and the exercise of faithful obedience to our Lord is opened. Truth understood in the heart is transformed to a power that gives life to others. Passions awaken and steadily nourished begin to determine our activity in the church and community. In a very real sense, we embody the continuing work of Jesus in the present day.

Silence the daily distractions, O Lord, which keeps me from pursuing a deeper relationship with you. Instill within me the desire to know you more fully and to participate more completely in your reconciling work in the world. Amen.

Adequate Faith

"The bed is too short to stretch out, and the shroud is too narrow to cover oneself."
Isaiah 28:20 (Common English Bible)

A bed that is too short and a blanket that is too narrow are inadequate for restful, healthy sleep. Both may serve us well as temporary arrangements when nothing else is available. But in the long term, either we find an adequate bed along with a sufficient blanket or we suffer; we will suffer general discomfort in our rest, experience aches and pains of every sort and possibly move through the day with sleep deprivation. Adequate rest requires adequate accommodation.

Just as a short bed fails to provide for a growing body and a narrow blanket leaves people shivering in the cold, so does a short and narrow faith leave us morally stunted and shivering with every kind of fear. God desires that we have a bed of faith on which to stretch a full human life and be warmly wrapped in the mantle of confidence in the living power of the risen Christ. When we hear of those who are short on integrity and frightened of every uncertainty, it is reasonable to ask the nature of the faith that is sustaining them.

Many who self-identify as Christians today live in the danger of believing too little. They are very uncomfortable on the beds of their faith. Ignoring the inevitable growing pains of faith, such people do little to nourish personal spiritual growth. They seek to make do with the cradle of faith provided them by others. The untroubled sleep of their early years now demands more – a larger bed of faith and a wider blanket of confidence in God. The faith question presses: Will they pursue a faith-growth plan that furnishes them with the largest and broadest and strongest thoughts of God that will sustain them as adults? Or will they continually seek to squeeze back into the crib in which they were so happy in childhood?

Perhaps there is nothing more pathetic than to see a Christian, who ought to be flexing an adult's faith in the challenges of life, content with a mere child's share of understanding of God. Instead of stretching onto an adult-sized faith, they tuck themselves into a cradle. Each morning they get up from it lame and aching. Worse, they are chilled by every blast of unbelief and uncertainty that blows.

Grant me the wisdom to seek you each day, O God, and the discipline to nurture faith practices that provide a faith sufficient for the challenges of life. Amen.

Authentic Faith

"And to love God with all of the heart, a full understanding, and all of one's strength, and to love one's neighbor as oneself is much more important than all kinds of entirely burned offerings and sacrifices."
Mark 12:33 (Common English Bible)

Burned offerings and sacrifices are not really a concern in the present-day church, at least not literally. Figuratively speaking, they are still very present. Today they simply look different. Perhaps you have noticed them on Sunday mornings during church. They show-up in a wide variety of disguises, the critical finger pointed at another's unwise clothing decision for coming to church, the haughty condemnation of another understanding of scripture, the boasting – subtle and less subtle – of service given to the ministry of the church. Each is an announcement that "my faith is better than your faith."

Jesus wasn't pleased with the burned offerings and sacrifices in His day; Jesus isn't pleased with them today. Perhaps it is because they are so powerful at drawing attention to the individual making the offering or sacrifice. And attention that is directed to the individual is attention not directed to Jesus.

It would be a mistake to conclude that our Lord simply isn't interested in sharing the stage with anyone else. No, what Jesus is up to is protecting each of us from conceit. Any grand and expansive gesture of sacrifice – or announcement of the stumbling of another – builds love for self while diminishing love for others. It is then that any practice of faith becomes a contest of whose journey is the better. Eventually, the whole notion of adoration of Jesus as Lord is replaced with the adoration of self. It becomes a faith that bears little resemblance to the Christian faith.

Jesus shows the way, in this one sentence, of authentic faith; a faith that honors God and glorifies Jesus. It is a faith that directs love to God and neighbor. It is a faith that cares deeply about something beyond the self. Loving God with all of one's heart, mind and strength and to love the neighbor just as ardently as we love ourselves demands considerable energy. Such love depletes resources that might be used for judgment of others and the aggrandizement of self. It is then that our faith ventures into the deeper places with Christ. It is then that faith realizes maturity.

Protect my heart, O God, from conceit. Replace judgment with love and graciousness. Use me as an instrument of your peace that Christ may be glorified in my thoughts and behavior. Amen.

Discerning Right from Wrong

"They are people who lack all sense of right and wrong."
Ephesians 4:19 (Common English Bible)

Imagine that most unfortunate condition! To be incapable of discerning what is right from what is wrong. It is a moral condition; a result when the capital of noble awareness and aspirations begins to shrink, and a person is brought into a state of spiritual bankruptcy. The ability to distinguish between right and wrong is less mental discernment than it is a moral sense. It is the spiritual palate which tests and discriminates the moral qualities of thoughts and actions. Indeed, Job, from the pages of the Old Testament, used this very figure of speech when he asked, "Can my mouth not recognize disaster?" (Job 6:30 CEB) Job knew wrong by its taste. He detected and found it distasteful, as the physical palate detects and rejects food that has spoiled.

A fine palate can lose its power of discernment. Particularly when the body is ill, the power of taste is often diminished or lost altogether. Certain medications used to treat physical symptoms can also result in the loss of taste. The person finds that all foods taste similar or there is no taste at all. Such people find they are incompetent to appreciate the delicate flavors once enjoyed of excellent cuisine. So let that same person neglect his spiritual condition and there is a similar result to the moral palate. Good and bad, right and wrong become mingled into a common insensitivity.

Attention to God is the oxygen of a vital, life-giving faith. Neglect the spiritual palate and the soul becomes drowsy. Then it becomes numb. After some time, any feeling of God is suffocated. Unable to distinguish one value from another, such people are driven by impulse. The dangerous result is that people turn themselves over to doing whatever feels good and to practicing every sort of corruption along with greed. Sin does it. Prayerlessness does it. Neglecting to regularly read God's Word and to meditate on it does it. God eventually seems absent.

The glory of our Savior is that he has defeated death – the physical kind. Placed in a tomb for three days, Jesus rose again and drew fresh breath into his lungs. Similarly, Jesus can fill our spiritual lungs with new breath and vitalize our spiritual nature. Jesus can restore a faith that has withered from neglect and restore sensitivity to our spiritual palate. A person who has lost all moral discernment can – by turning again to God – recover all sense of right and wrong and know the pulse, and taste, of life as God intends.

Abundant God, you cause water to flow in desert places and bring life from parched ground. Release within my soul the springs of life-giving waters that I may always discern your most perfect will and taste and see that you are good. Amen.

Misreading the Bible

"Therefore, if you worship me, it will all be yours."
Luke 4:7 (Common English Bible)

Catherine Cavazos Renken, Presbyterian pastor and friend, recently posted on Facebook a page from a Christian inspirational calendar, presumably one that she had used in a previous year. The Bible selection for Thursday, July 3rd reads, *"Therefore, if you worship me, it will all be yours."* It was an unfortunate selection by the publishers of the daily calendar. As Catherine notes in her posting, "Inspirational Bible Quote Less Inspirational If You Know Who Said It." A cursory reading of this verse in the Bible quickly makes apparent that these words are spoken by Satan to Jesus – a small portion of Satan's temptation of Jesus while Jesus was on a mountaintop in prayer.

Removed from context, nearly anyone can use selected scripture to advance their own political position, ideology or religious convictions. Scripture is used to bar women from leadership in the church, was used to support slavery and often used to discriminate against anyone who fails to hold a particular – and narrow – interpretation of God's Word. It seems to me that such use of the Bible is less concerned with advancing God's Kingdom and more concerned with advancing the kingdom of the individual. As that great teacher of the faith, Paul Tillich once remarked, "The Bible is God's Word not when you think you can grasp it but when you allow it to grasp you."

The question becomes, on whose terms do we seek to interpret the Bible – the Bible or ours? Critical study and interpretation of the Bible in its historical and cultural context is often dismissed if conclusions differ with cherished notions of understanding. Bumper stickers that declare, "The Bible says it, I believe it, end of conversation" often betray a mind closed to deeper insights of an authentic and genuine witness of the Bible. Surely, such persons wouldn't apply a literal interpretation to Psalm 137:9, "A blessing on the one who seizes your children and smashes them against the rock!"

Present in the fifth chapter of Acts there is a Pharisee and teacher of the faith named Gamaliel, well respected by all the people. He is present when the early apostles of the Christian faith are being ridiculed and harassed due to their teaching and preaching of the risen Christ. Simply, the apostles' interpretation of the faith is rejected. The "religious establishment" of the day was furious at the apostles and wanted to kill them. Gamaliel urged restraint – "what if the apostles are right? You will then find yourselves fighting God!" His counsel is sound today. Perhaps more civility in our speech and humility of heart would be wise as we consider the reading – and hearing – of God's Word today by those who stand in a different place than us.

Grant me the humility of heart and the civility of speech that I may recognize new truths and new understandings as I follow Jesus today. Amen.

Looking Back, Looking Forward

"Watch yourself! Don't forget the Lord, who brought you out of Egypt, out of the house of slavery."
Deuteronomy 6:12 (Common English Bible)

Temple University of Philadelphia is currently promoting their educational opportunities with the moniker, *Always Charging Forward*. I imagine that it is effective – tapping into our natural propensity to look at the life that stretches out ahead of us. With an education from Temple University we are empowered to charge – with considerable power – into what lies ahead rather than merely stumbling into it. Obsessed with the future as we are today, many are prepared to invest considerable resources to take advantage of every opportunity that presents a better quality of life. Temple University wants us to believe that it all starts with an education that they can provide.

Confidence in an unknown future requires considerable planning, preparation and faith. For the Christian, faith usually means that our future is in the hands of an almighty God and that God can be trusted to see us into that future and through it. That point of view is sound in our Christian understanding of God's activity. But the writer of Deuteronomy wants us to know that it is inadequate. Faith is deeper and richer than our confidence in what God will do. Faith is also looking over our shoulder at what God has done. "Watch yourself! Don't forget the Lord, who brought you out of Egypt, out of the house of slavery."

Some today ask, "Why go to church and listen to all that stuff about the distant past; about ancient Israel and Egypt?" "What do the characters of Abraham and Moses have to do with us?" What they are really declaring is that they seek a faith that is up-to-date, a faith for the future. Yet, those same people will acknowledge that they have faith in America primarily because of our nation's history. It is because we believe that certain things have happened that we have confidence in what can happen. Confidence – or faith – doesn't simply leap from nowhere.

So the writer of Deuteronomy asks that we look back in faith before we look forward. There are moments in our past that are quite decisive for us, moments that provide a foundation of confidence for that forward-looking faith that we so desperately seek. To look back in faith is how we refresh our memory of God's power and faithfulness. That is what provides the sturdy base for trust and hope today. This is why the people of God gather, week after week, to worship – to recall the old, old story of God's faithfulness that empowers our charging forward into the future.

Lord Jesus, ignite in me the desire to explore more deeply the rich stories of faith that they may direct my steps today and all of my tomorrows. Amen.

The Allure of a Defeated Life

"I was given a thorn in my body."
2 Corinthians 12:7 (Common English Bible)

Few things are as unfortunate as to see a woman or man losing heart and all sense of hope, drifting into apathy, and finally despair. When a sense of defeat is permitted to take residence in a life, frustration and inaction are too frequently the result. The face becomes sullen, the head is held low, and the shoulders sag. Bitterness grows, the result of an erroneous belief that life has dealt a raw deal or that others have received better opportunities. Left unchecked, the self-pity sentences them to low levels of achievement. A strange comfort is found in simply giving-up – experiencing a certain allure of being defeated.

History is replete with men and women who have experienced hardship, anguished over setbacks, and struggled with handicaps – physical, mental and emotional. Anyone of them may have been resentful and rebellious – and many have – with bad behavior the consequence. Yet, there are others who rise above the circumstances of their lives, press forward with unbelievable determination and consecrate their lives to the service of others. The apostle Paul stands among them. Paul moved through life hindered by "a thorn in the body" but produced nearly two-thirds of our New Testament.

Rather than giving-up and accepting defeat, Paul labored under his handicap. Naturally, Paul – like any of us – preferred that the handicap be corrected, the difficulty removed. On three occasions Paul asked the Lord for this. But the handicap remained; the thorn wasn't removed. But Paul's prayers were answered. "My grace is enough for you," answered God. With God's answer, Paul committed himself to do the very best he could do with what he had. His life and ministry were a vessel of hope for everyone he encountered. To his children, Theodore Roosevelt continually cultivated a hopeful disposition – and in doing so charged the atmosphere of his home with hope.

Paul sought to demonstrate in his life that there is no limitation, no misfortune, no burden of sorrow, suffering or loss that the human spirit cannot rise above. He endured much of each. But Paul went deeper than self-discipline and self-determination. Paul triumphed over it all because he sought God. Perhaps this was the finest message that Paul left the church – that when the allure of defeat tempts the heart Paul calls us to that deeper place where our life is open to the grace and power of Almighty God.

Heavenly Father, forgive me when I choose hopelessness rather than hope, despair rather than confidence in your love when confronted with difficulty. Amen.

Treasure in Clay Pots

"But we have this treasure in clay pots so that the awesome power belongs to God and doesn't come from us."
2 Corinthians 4:7 (Common English Bible)

My favorite photographer today is Alan S. Maltz. His work is primarily nature, destination and landscape photography with particular attention on South Florida. His work has garnered wide acclaim including *The Official Wildlife Photographer of Florida* by The Wildlife Foundation of Florida and *The Official Fine Art Photographer of Florida* by Visit Florida. His work is not inexpensive so, consequently, I have only one of his pieces, <u>Tropical Blues</u>, a lovely sunset in the Florida Keys.

I purchased this piece already matted but unframed. This is how I have displayed it in my office for nearly two years – waiting until I am comfortable in spending an extravagant sum to have it properly framed. Though there will be some who may disagree with me, I believe that it is not fitting to enclose such a lovely – and expensive – picture in an inexpensive frame. Priceless artifacts are encased in lovely and prominent cabinets in museums and expensive jewelry is placed in presentation boxes that are nearly as beautiful as the jewelry itself. Anything less would fail to properly value the artifact or beautiful jewelry. The same is true for this rich and beautiful photograph. Yet this, writes Paul, is precisely what God has done.

In a startling contrast, God has taken the magnificent treasure of divine grace and placed it in human hearts – hearts that are likened to clay pots. This is a God who would take a fine art photograph of Alan S. Maltz and place it quickly into a tawdry picture frame found in a yard sale. Here is an immense and glorious treasure entrusted to such broken and pathetic instruments as men and women; jewels of a great Kingdom placed in a flimsy box of cardboard. *"But we have this treasure in clay pots."* This is what God has done – and so, there must be a lesson here for all of us.

Paul invites the reader to join him in discovery, to find the reason and purpose for this most unusual contrast of treasure and clay. And Paul's rich discovery is our discovery: *"so that the awesome power belongs to God and doesn't come from us."* God's purpose is that it will be unmistakable to the world that the forward movement of the church's mission cannot be credited to us, the church. The power of the church to change lives and transform communities does not come from human strength and determination. Anyone who has an honest estimation of human ability understands that. They understand that, alone, any of us are inadequate for the job. There must be something more, something else at work in us to accomplish the immense task of making whole in the world what is broken. That something more, that something else is God.

Gracious God, I ask that I may be used by you today in such manner that others will see the presence of the risen and living Christ within me. Amen.

When Faith Is Difficult

"We can't find goodness anywhere."
Psalm 4:6 (Common English Bible)

If there remains anyone who argues that the Bible isn't relevant for today, they have demonstrated that they haven't paid attention to the Bible – not close attention anyway. Is there anything more timeless than the agonizing cry, "We can't find goodness anywhere?" Each morning our minds are disturbed by the growing threat of the militant Islamic group, ISIS, the conflict between Israel and Palestine and the racial unrest in Ferguson, Missouri. Beneath these attention getting headlines is the less mentioned but continuing concern of the growing wealth gap in our country and the millions in our nation who struggle daily to simply have enough. There are no snappy answers to the painful question of human struggle.

It is well that the Bible does not offer a quick and pre-fabricated answer to this despairing cry. And it is best for us to refrain from such a temptation. First, we are not free to indulge in any cynical or dismissal attitudes such as, "Well, that's life," or, "Bad things just happen." As followers of Jesus we are baptized into the common confession that our lives are in the hands of God, and that this God is a God of love. Second, we don't occupy some place between God and the struggle of humanity. Not one of us has some special insight into the mysterious work of God in the midst of our common difficulty. Each of us must sweat it out with everyone else.

What remains is a prayer: "Lord, show us once more the light of your face." This is the prayer of the Psalmist and nothing new can be added. The prayer is the same today as it was yesterday, fresh and urgent. It is as new as the earthquake that shook the San Francisco Bay Area a few days ago and the agony that kept someone awake last night. It is new when we utter it personally, today. No devotional, not one inspirational book can answer the plea, the emotional depth of that prayer.

On our knees we pray. If we listen in the silences between our words, the Holy Spirit reminds us that God was never absent in the horrors of human life in the Bible – nor will God be absent today. On the

Via Dolorosa – the way of the cross – in Jerusalem, God was very present in the heart of human misery giving, giving and giving himself, so that after this there would be no fear, no despair and no doubt of God's love. The cry, "We can't find goodness anywhere," still sounds in the streets of our communities. We live with it and we hear it echo in our souls. But the Spirit helps us recall the suffering of Christ – a suffering accepted out of Christ's love for us. It is a love that will work for the good of all those who love him.

In moments when my heart grows weary, help me remember the Via Dolorosa, the way of the cross. In the certain name of Jesus, I pray. Amen.

Victory on Our Knees

"I live on high, in holiness, and also with the crushed and the lowly, reviving the spirit of the lowly, reviving the heart of those who have been crushed."
Isaiah 57:15 (Common English Bible)

Recently Grace and I spent a weekend in the Florida Keys with two dear friends. In addition to sharing meals together, shopping, stimulating conversation about our families and an evening of bicycling, the four of us summoned the courage to try something we had never done before – paddle boarding. Popularity of the sport seems to be growing exponentially in South Florida, particularly the Keys. It looked fun and appeared to be a sport that would be easy for beginners. It was not. Paddle boarding challenges both core strength and balance and beginners spend more time falling from the board than standing. My wife, Grace, perhaps an exception; other people asking me how long she had been paddle boarding.

After several attempts at standing – and failing – Grace said to me to begin on my knees, "you have more control on your knees." Hearing my wife's words, my friend commented, "I hear a sermon in there somewhere!" Naturally, I was frustrated that I was unable to master paddle boarding immediately. But then, where would have been the satisfaction in that? Satisfaction of life is often preceded by considerable effort and discipline. So it is with our Christian faith. We must experience failure on our own before we can value God's presence and strength that enables us to stand. The pinnacle of joy and satisfaction in our faith is our communion with the Risen Christ. That communion begins on our knees in prayer – our demonstration that we can't do life apart from God.

To be a Christian is to follow Jesus. And his own life was no leap from the cradle in Bethlehem to the victory of Easter morning. Victory implies something was defeated. Between birth and resurrection, Jesus lived deeply. It was a life that knew suffering, betrayal and abandonment. We experience with Jesus the victory and joy of the Resurrection because we know all too well his hell of loneliness and pain. It was a hell that Jesus defeated because he spent so much of his life on his knees. Grace is absolutely right, "You have more control on your knees."

The central question that confronts many today is where is God in the darkness of the present world – the darkness that seems to defeat a hope for tomorrow? Isaiah declares that our God lives with the crushed and the lowly. God is not only present in our darkness; God is at work, "reviving the spirit of the lowly, reviving the heart of those who have been crushed." God did so for Jesus. God will do so for us. What is needed is that we wait for God's victory on our knees.

Holy Spirit, stir me and ready me for inspiration when the verdict of the day seems to suggest there remains little hope. Amen.

The Puzzle of Prayer

"We always thank God for all of you when we mention you constantly in our prayers."
1 Thessalonians 1:2 (Common English Bible)

It is not unusual for someone to ask me, "Please pray for me." Often my response is an invitation to immediate prayer. My desire is to take the request for prayer seriously. By praying with the person immediately, I wish to say that I care deeply about them and that I appreciate their confidence in the power of prayer. Recently, however, I have begun to question, "Just what do they expect from this prayer?" "Do they really believe my prayer to do any good?"

Naturally, the Bible has much to say about prayer. What is often unrealized is just how frequently the mention of prayer in the Bible is one of complaint. The palmists, the prophets, Job and the apostle Paul often questioned the value of prayer, sometimes rather bluntly! Listen to a portion of Psalm 88, "But I cry out to you, Lord! My prayer meets you first thing in the morning! Why do you reject my very being, Lord? Why do you hide your face from me (verse 13, 14)?" It is clear that today's church is not the first to question the usefulness of prayer.

It is important – and helpful – to note, however, that in each complaint that is uttered there is present a fervent belief that something can be expected from prayer. Prayer is never given up on in the Bible, never dismissed as not of any use. What makes each of those who wrestle with prayer people of amazing stature is their absolute confidence in the power of prayer – power to disrupt at any moment the ordinary with the extraordinary. Without reserve or embarrassment each character in the Bible shared in the same compulsion to pray.

I will freely share that I have no idea how prayer works. The question itself may be foolish simply because it strives to understand God. And someone once wisely declared that if we can ever grasp God then we must go looking for another God. Any God we can understand with our finite minds is simply too small to save us. What I am confident of is that God was very active in the drama recorded in the Bible and continues to be just as involved in the unfolding drama of life today. And God invites us, repeatedly, to seek the inflowing of God's grace through regular prayer. Refusal to pray – even when prayer was questioned –simply was not an option for the people of faith in the Bible.

Heavenly Father, we pray today for one another. Grant your grace to each one as they have need, and strengthen our faith, particularly in moments when you seem silent. Amen.

The Full Development of Faith

"I want to do your will, my God."
Psalm 40:8 (Common English Bible)

Spring training, 2015 will find Giancarlo Stanton suited-up as a Miami Marlin. Signed to a thirteen-year, $325 million-dollar contract – more money than any other American athlete in a single contract – Stanton was not easily convinced that this was the right move in his career. The contract offered Stanton was unprecedented in both length and value. If money alone was the determining factor, it was a clear decision. It wasn't. Ben Reiter writes in the current issue of *Sport's Illustrated* that Stanton is "driven by something else: a desire to wring everything he could out of his gifted body. So he has pushed himself to become an all-around force."[2] Naturally, that personal drive could be pursued with any MLB franchise. Where Stanton played baseball would be driven by something higher than the pursuit of personal wealth.

A life that reaches for something higher than personal gain is rare and spacious. Here, in this Psalm, the one who writes declares that they desire to do God's will. This marks a mature stage in discipleship. Listen to many prayers today and what is heard is a plea that God honors the will of the individual. These are not the prayers of a life fully consecrated to God. To address God at all in prayer indicates the presence of a faith journey. But such a journey is not complete until there is absent any desire except God's will.

Prayers of those new to the faith naturally begin with requests for oneself. This is not altogether a bad thing. Prayer itself indicates the presence of trust in a God who is concerned and desires our good. Even the prayer taught us by our Lord - the Lord's Prayer - includes a personal request, "Give us the bread we need for today." (Matthew 6:11 Common English Bible) After faith begins to experience growth there is noticed some constraint and reluctance in making personal requests known to God. The growing faith becomes inclined to know God and God's will.

It is here, in this simple prayer of the Psalmist, *"I want to do your will, my God,"* that faith reaches full development. What at first was constrained has come at length to be natural. The heart is fixed on nothing less than pleasing God. The bent of life is God-ward where the best of everything abides. It is here that we become what we were created to be - more fully human and less self-centered. And the responsive service of our life to others is broadened.

My prayer today, Lord, is that my own heart may be as that of John the Baptist when he said, "I must decrease and he (Jesus) must increase." Amen.

---

[2]Ben Reiter, "Miami Masterpiece." *Sports Illustrated.* March 2, 2015, pages 46-53.

The Silent Word

"Because of his powerful deeds and words, he was recognized by God and all the people as a prophet."
Luke 24:19 (Common English Bible)

I was told this week that a member of the church I have served for better than two years somehow has the notion that the regular reading of the Bible isn't important. They do read each day a devotional provided by the church and that devotional does have a sentence of scripture provided prior to each meditation – much like the one you are reading now. But that is all. The Bible remains a closed book in their home. It is unimaginable that this person listens to me each week and concludes that reading the Bible is unimportant.

The words you are reading now are human words. The words of the devotional mentioned above are human words. Certainly, I hope that these words are helpful in directing people to the one, Holy Word that is the Bible. It is my prayer that my words here each week provide some deeper insight and understanding to God's Word. Yet, I submit, my words – or any human words – are not an adequate substitute for God's Word recorded in the Bible. Only the Bible is capable of communicating "the silent word."

"The silent word" that I speak of here is that unspoken word that is heard in the heart. It is that word spoken by the Holy Spirit to convey the reality of God with an imagination and force that human words are incapable. It is a word that has uncommon resonance with the particulars of our daily life: the myriad little and large decisions that press for our attention each day. God certainly uses the stumbling human words of women and men to help convey the silent word of God's kingdom. But it is God's Word in the Bible that has a unique power to bring the silent word to life in our hearts. It is a word that ultimately silences our chatter and confronts us with the living word that is Christ.

In this sentence of scripture from the Gospel of Luke, Jesus is presented as a prophet that is powerful in deeds and words. The mighty deeds and the mighty words Jesus spoke were inseparable. With considerable force, Luke seeks to be clear that Jesus' words were not less important than Jesus' deeds. When a paralyzed man was brought to Jesus for healing, his first act was the spoken word, "Your sins are forgiven." Luke wants us to understand that when God's Word is spoken - or read - the silent word finds lodgment in the human heart. Sooner or later, that silent word accomplishes what no human word can, it conforms us to the image of Christ.

Implant your word deeply into my heart, O God, that I may know your will more clearly and love you and others more deeply. In Christ's name, I ask. Amen.

Something Familiar

"Then the two disciples described what had happened along the road and how Jesus was made known to them as he broke the bread."
Luke 24: 35 (Common English Bible)

This week I received Brian Wilson's new album, No Pier Pressure, his eleventh solo album. It is heavy on guest stars including Zooey Deschanel, my favorite guest on the album. Together, Wilson and Deschanel sing a track called, *On the Island*, a breezy lounge tune that imagines becoming stranded in the Caribbean. After listening to this track several times alone I asked my wife to listen and guess who Brian Wilson is singing with. Before the first lyric was sung she answered, Zooey Deschanel! "How could you possibly know that? No one has started singing!" I said. "The whistling," my wife answered. "Zooey Deschanel's whistling is familiar to me." Indeed, the track begins with whistling before the first lyric is sung.

Here, in Luke's Gospel it is Easter, now later in the day from the experience of the resurrection that morning. Two disciples are walking together along a road, traveling to a village called Emmaus, about seven miles from Jerusalem. They were talking to each other about everything that had happened in the past few days; the parade into Jerusalem, the arrest and the crucifixion of Jesus. While they were discussing these things, Jesus appears and joins them in their journey. But, they did not recognize that it was Jesus.

Jesus asks the disciples what they are talking about. With brokenness and grief, they express their astonishment that anyone would have to ask, "Are you the only visitor to Jerusalem who is unaware of the things that have taken place there over the last few days?" (Verse 18) The disciples then proceed to tell "this stranger" all that had occurred. More, they express that their deepest hope had been that the one crucified would be the promised one to redeem Israel. After arriving in Emmaus Jesus pretended to leave the disciples and continue on. But they urged him to stay and share supper with them. After Jesus took his place at the table he took bread, blessed it and broke it. At that moment the two disciples recognized Jesus! Why did they recognize Jesus at that precise moment? According to the Bible, there was something familiar in how Jesus took the bread, blessed it and broke it.

The question that presses against my heart when I read this story is this; will anyone recognize me today as a follower of Jesus? Will there be anything familiar in how I speak, how I behave and the manner in which I love that will result in others seeing Jesus in me? The Christian life has much more to do with our lives than with a mental consent to a collection of thoughts and beliefs. The Christian life is a call to a reorientation of how we are to live. It is a call to an imitation of the life of Jesus. Our progress will be measured when others recognize something familiar in us, something that reminds them of Jesus.

Heavenly Father, you meant that my faith should be alive and vital, full of wonder and power. Give me today a vision of how you intend to use me for your purposes that I may experience a full maturity of faith, even to the full stature of Christ. Amen.

God's Desire

"Which commandment is the most important of all?' Jesus replied, 'The most important one is Israel, listen! Our God is one Lord, and you must love the Lord your God with all your heart, with all your being, with all your mind, and with all your strength. The second is this, you will love your neighbor as yourself.'"
Mark 12:28b-31 (Common English Bible)

The question, "Which commandment is the most important of all?" is telling, even indicting. The question discloses the human heart that continually seeks, with considerable eagerness, to advance in personal stature by right belief and acts of piety. It is a question that is less concerned for another. The concern is for self and doing all that is necessary to be held in high esteem by others. So, what is sought is an understanding of the rank and priority of scale of God's laws. With this knowledge is the ability to focus behavior for maximum value in the sight of God – it is the striving for self-righteousness. Are we to do this first or the other?

Of course, this isn't the only place we see this condition of the human heart. Jesus addresses this on multiple occasions, most notably in the sixth chapter of Matthew's Gospel, "Be careful that you don't practice your religion in front of people to draw their attention. If you do, you will have no reward from your Father who is in heaven (verse 1)." Such behavior – or condition of the heart – misses the aim of God's story. What God desires is "to do justice, embrace faithful love, and walk humbly with your God (Micah 6:8)." Striving to please God by demonstrations of piety is devoid of any semblance of humility.

God's desire is not for sacrifices and human scrambling for an esteemed position among God's people. Instead, God's pleasure is dwelling with humanity and abiding together as God leads us into a deeper understanding and embrace of love – love for God and love for neighbor. More, God is more than a participant in this covenantal community; God is the prime sustainer and most glorious inhabitant. The resurrection of Jesus marks the end of self-righteousness.

Jesus' answer to the question, "Which commandment is the most important of all?" is a call to unshackle ourselves from a faith that values right belief and outward acts of piety over transformed hearts, lives, and communities. God's concern is about life together, not one's personal stature. Anything else marginalizes the central message and objective of Jesus – the call to right relationships – and imprisons once again the human heart in ceaseless striving to earn favor with God. Walk in love, teaches Jesus, and in this walk the truth of God's Kingdom will have its finest witness.

So saturate me with the experience of your love that your love may overflow from me to everyone I meet today. Amen.

Why?

"We can't find goodness anywhere."
Psalm 4:6 (Common English Bible)

It would seem that the one who wrote these words has been paying attention to our daily news. After skimming the headlines of the morning paper or turning off the nightly news these seem to be our words; "We can't find goodness anywhere." A plane crash that kills everyone on board, religious extremist who take innocent lives, and violence in our cities – is any of that good? There are many who are weary; many who would ask, isn't there anything good for us to see?

The mood here is one of desperation. This is a plea for someone, anyone, to show us something good – to point to the light in the darkness. And the darkness seems vast. Yet, though we may seek a pile of ready-made answers, the Bible does not provide them. Snappy answers or smooth arguments to the agonizing question of human experience are absent. All that remains is this plea before God. But that is something. A plea before God is an affirmation of faith that there is God. There may be darkness in the world. But God is also in the world.

We may ask, "Why God would let something like this happen?" I received that very question this week in my email box. Yet, we must know that this is not the first time this question has been seriously raised. This is a question that stretches forward to us from the beginning of human sin. And there is our best clue to our question; human sin. All of humanity participates in a rebellion against God's good purposes. It is that rebellion – both individual and corporate – that results in brokenness and hurt to others. The cross of Jesus is the central symbol of our faith because it reminds us that much happens in our world that is outside of God's good desire for us. But God is in the world, and through the cross, seeks to reclaim this world stained and broken by sin

The God of love is not absent in this world filled with bad news. The cross demonstrates that God is right in the middle of it. More, the cross powerfully reminds us that even in the midst of our active rebellion, even while we are sinners, God dies for us. Who does that?

Who dies for someone who is hurling their worst behavior at you? This Holy Week we are given that answer once again.

In moments of doubt, confusion, and despair, may I remember the certainty of your presence, concern, and love demonstrated in the cross of your Son, Jesus. Amen.

When Our Hearts Are Anxious

"Don't be anxious about anything; rather bring up all of your requests to God in your prayers and petitions, along with giving thanks."
Philippians 4:6 (Common English Bible)

There seems to be no shortage of excruciating stresses, interpersonal struggles and reasons to be anxious. Some are better than others in putting on a brave face, but their demeanor hides what we all know is a fact of life – life is difficult. And many days we find it a struggle simply to push through ordinary chores and responsibilities. A heart heavy with anxiety is exhausting.

The careful reader of the Bible will notice that anxiety and worry are mentioned often. This is good news because it says that anxious hearts matter to God. Certainly, it is important to the Apostle Paul. He writes in this sentence of scripture that we are not to be anxious about anything. The difficulty, of course, is that saying is one thing. Doing is quite another matter.

Fortunately, Paul doesn't simply slap us on the back, admonish us not to worry and leave it at that. What Paul does is offer an antidote for anxious hearts: *"rather bring up all of your requests to God in your prayers and petitions, along with giving thanks."* Paul is asking that we make God a partner with everything that weighs so heavily on us. Giving voice to those things that trouble us goes a long way in reducing their grip on our lives. Yet, Paul's advice is more than simply talking about our problems. Paul tells us additionally to give thanks; to remember in the midst of our anxiety that God has been faithful in the past and to realize that past performance does indicate the promise of continued faithfulness.

Some years ago, a pastor in New York City would conclude his prayers by saying, *"Help us to lean back into the strong arms of Jesus Christ. Amen."* Paul is saying the same thing here. Paul is not denying the power of anxiety. There was no shortage of anxious moments in his ministry. What Paul is asking that we do is remember the faithfulness of God in our past and then to lean into that same faithfulness now when our hearts become heavy. There is no promise that our problems will all go away. What Paul promises is God's peace.

In my own anxious moments, O Lord, remind me of your continued love and care for me. Settle my heart and help me to lean back on the strong arms of Jesus. It is in his name I pray. Amen.

Uniola paniculata (Sea Oats)

"...it's not you that sustains the root, but it's the root that sustains you."
Romans 11:18b (Common English Bible)

Sea oats is an extremely valuable plant for coastline and barrier island protection. Drought-tolerant sea oats produces a massive root system that firmly holds loose soil and sand in place during extreme weather. Additionally, due to its expansive and long root structure, sea oats are capable of catching blowing sand and building dunes. As such, sea oats are an important part of natural and artificial dune stabilization during tropical storms and hurricanes. In Fort Lauderdale, a colony of sea oats has been planted as a crucial component of that city's hurricane beach defense strategy.

The next time you are enjoying the beach, pay attention to this beautiful grass commonly found in the upper dunes along beach fronts. Growing erect up to six feet in height with leaves that can reach twenty-four inches in length, it would be easy to mistakenly believe that it is the beach that sustains life for this plant. This simply isn't the case. It is the root structure of sea oats that sustains the beautiful beach.

This is similar to what Paul is saying here in his letter to the church in Rome. Many non-Jewish people have now come to believe in Jesus Christ. On the one hand, this is good news. God's Kingdom is growing as deep as the roots of sea oats and just as pervasive. On the other hand, some of these non-Jewish followers of Jesus are growing smug. Paul has heard that they are boasting that their faith is responsible for their identity as God's people. With this belief is the tendency to look down on those we are quite sure are not saved, particularly non-believing Jews. Be careful, warns Paul. We belong to God, not because of our godliness, our faith, but despite our ungodliness. God chose us before we chose God. And God chose the Jewish people first.

New followers of Jesus are indebted, even dependent, on the spiritual heritage of the Old Testament people of God. Paul uses his now famous analogy to advance this point. Non-Jewish believers are like wild olive branches that have been grafted alongside the natural branches, the Jewish people; the early Jewish leaders of the faith are the root. If God has shown mercy to us who are not the natural branches, how much more may God one day show mercy to the people of Israel, who are the natural branches who do not yet believe. As Paul states, it is not we, new followers of Jesus, who sustain the faith. It is the root, the people of Israel who sustain us.

Forgive our arrogance and replace it with humility. Strengthen our understanding of your mercy and direct us in speech and behavior that honors the life and ministry of Jesus Christ. Amen.

Flags on the Beach

"But if you do warn the righteous not to sin, and they don't sin, they will be declared righteous. Their lives will be preserved because they heeded the warning, and you will save your life."
Ezekiel 3:21 (Common English Bible)

The sky is clear, and the temperature is optimal for a day at the beach. You grab your sunscreen, a chair and a good book and look forward to a day in the sun, sand and surf. After making your way along the path that has been cleared through the sea grapes and other natural coastal fauna, you arrive on the beach and discover that flags have been prominently placed on or near lifeguard stations. Someone has been given the responsibility for flying the correct flag for each day's swimming conditions. Though there may be some regional differences, the flag warning system is used by coastal communities worldwide to alert beach goers of potential water hazards.

On Delray Beach there are ordinarily four-color flags. Green flags are the most welcomed. They are flown when the day is clear, and the water is calm. A green flag is an all clear sign - safe to swim and enjoy the day. Yellow flags mean that ocean conditions are not optimal but not life-threatening. There may be a high surf or dangerous current and caution is advised. A purple flag indicates that dangerous marine life is in the water or on the shore. This flag may be flown with other flags and suggests extreme caution. Red flags are the most serious. Usually, a red flag is used to discourage swimming by all but very strong swimmers.

Ezekiel is given "flag duty" by God for the people of Israel. He must shoulder the responsibility of placing warning flags in their midst alerting them of God's presence and claim upon their lives. Whether the people paid attention to the flags or not was not Ezekiel's concern, only that he got the word out. If the people were wise and heeded the warnings, they would live. Otherwise, they would perish. It is a considerable responsibility to discern the day's conditions and carefully raise the appropriate flag.

As members of a faith community we have a similar responsibility. That responsibility is not necessarily to walk around announcing dire warnings. Rather, it is a responsibility to make a positive investment in the lives of others. As Ezekiel, God calls us to take an interest in the common welfare of others, to pour ourselves into their lives in such a manner that they see God and God's care for them. By our genuine interest in others, we deliver ourselves from an inward focus that only results in selfishness, meanness and, ultimately fear of loss. It is how we will save our own lives.

Heavenly Father, make me alert today of those around me that I may invest my time, gifts and energy into that they may know you and experience the riches of faith in Jesus Christ. Amen.

Sandcastles

"But everybody who hears these words of mine and doesn't put them into practice will be like a fool who built a house on sand. The rain fell, the floods came, and the wind blew and beat against that house. It fell and was completely destroyed."
Matthew 7:26, 27 (Common English Bible)

He is known as Mr. Sandman. Mark Mason traded his high-paying career in sales to make sandcastles. From every indication, he is doing very well with his new vocation. A recent issue of *Islands* magazine reports that companies like Disney and Coca-Cola hire Mark and his crew – Team Sandcastle – to build custom sand sculptures, some going for more than $100,000 a pop. Additionally, Mark's team builds sculptures for major personal events like wedding proposals. People are surprised when they learn that "building sandcastles" is Mark's profession. Mark understands. He told Sarah Sekula, writer for *Islands* magazine that he thinks the same thing. "It's just crazy cool!"[3]

Mark understands, of course, that everything he builds today has a very short life. Sandcastles crumble. High-tide, rain, wind and multiple other factors quickly and effectively remove all traces of Mark's skillful creations. Regardless of the size of the sculpture or its complexity, each one is temporary. It is simply the nature of the building material of choice. Some sand has greater firmness than other sand. Mark's preference is for the sand of the Bahamas with Grand Cayman a close second. But sand is sand. Eventually, it all washes away.

Matthew asks that we consider carefully the material we select when we build our life. Specifically, Matthew asks that we look closely at our foundation of choice when we build. Sand is a poor choice. Rain will fall, floods will appear, and the wind will blow and beat against our lives. These things are inevitable, says Matthew. So consider carefully how you will build. We may build a life every bit as spectacular as the sculptures of Mr. Sandman. But if they are built on a foundation of sand, that life is only temporary. Such a life cannot stand in the storms of life.

There is a place for sandcastles. They are sometimes extraordinary and cause delight to beachgoers. But a sandy lot is no place to build a life. A life of greed is one built on a sandy lot. A life of immediate gratification and self-indulgence is one built on a sandy lot. A life of power and position or arrogance is a life built on a sandy lot. Rigid adherence to one political position without appreciating another viewpoint can be a sandy lot. Any of these may seem lovely for a moment. But torrential downpours will wipe it all away. The wise not only pay attention to God's Word, each day they secure the foundation of their lives by that word. And theirs will be a dwelling that even the greatest storms of life cannot shake.

Sandy lots are so appealing, O God. Forgive me when I seek to build my life upon wealth, arrogance or anything else but your holy word in the Bible. Amen.

---

[3]Sarah Sekula, "Mr. Sandman: This is his livelihood." *Islands*. May 2015, page 47.

Beachcombing

"I consider everything a loss in comparison with the superior value of knowing Christ Jesus my Lord. I have lost everything for him, but what I lost I think of as sewer trash, so that I might gain Christ."
Philippians 3:8 (Common English Bible)

Beachcombing has become one my favorite activities that I share with my wife. The treasure that is freely presented by the sea changes with every wave that washes ashore. Rare pieces of sea glass, interesting stones and shells, and the occasional piece of driftwood provide a most fascinating diversion from the daily tasks and responsibilities that can consume any of us. Collecting unusual pieces and sharing what I have found with my wife helps me unwind and slip out of my day-to-day routine. Worries fade for both of us as we become caught-up in the fascination of discovery.

There is also trash and dangerous sea life that washes ashore. Broken glass with sharp edges and jellyfish tends to present the greatest danger to bare feet on the beach. Most beaches provide a purple flag to alert those walking the edge of the surf to the presence of dangerous sea life. This is helpful, of course, but the eye must remain sharp to see other harmful items that wash ashore such as nails, needles and sharp pieces of metal. Placing the bare foot upon any of these changes one's mood and diminishes an otherwise beautiful day. Worries that had faded are replaced with other worries.

What is important is developing a sharp eye to discern between treasure and trash, what is a collectable and what is dangerous. Our spiritual lives require the same discernment. What we collect in life will either draw us closer to God or lead us away. Particularly in the midst of the craziness of life, busy schedules and the need to multitask, we must exercise care to carry God with us. Otherwise, we may discover one day that we have spent our life gathering those things that have little value. Worse, we may realize that we completely missed the true treasure – a life-filling relationship with Jesus.

Paul doesn't want us to miss the treasure. So he makes a sharp distinction between what he once considered valuable and now knowing Christ. By comparison to Christ Jesus, everything else is little more than "sewer trash". Perhaps this is hyperbole. Perhaps it isn't. What is important is that as Paul walks the shores of life, he now understands the difference between what has value and what doesn't. And he urgently wants us to know the same.

Dear Lord, it is so easy to mistake trash for treasure, to spend our lives gathering the wrong things. By the instruction of your word each day, direct my vision to those things that have true value. Amen.

Sea Glass

"My brothers and sisters, think of the various tests you encounter as occasions for joy. After all, you know that the testing of your faith produces endurance. Let this endurance complete its work so that you may be fully mature, complete, and lacking in nothing."
James 1:2-4 (Common English Bible)

Since moving to south Florida from Pennsylvania one year ago, my wife, Grace has developed a new hobby, collecting sea glass from the beach. Finding sea glass often requires a careful eye and quick reflexes to collect from the coastline before a wave washes it away. But the effort is handsomely rewarded. Sea glass is simply beautiful and makes even more beautiful and rather expensive jewelry.

Sea glass begins as normal shards of broken glass. Bottles, jars and even fine china that in ordinary use become shattered, are discarded into the ocean. Years and years of persistent tumbling in the depths of the sea, often for fifty years or more, results in a smoothing and rounding of the sharp edges. Additionally, this process transforms the once slick surface of the glass to a beautiful frosted appearance. It is this rather turbulent and long process that produces such beauty. Naturally, no two pieces are ever identical, making each one a unique treasure.

James, the brother of Jesus, invites us to re-imagine the various trials and difficulties we encounter in life. Much like sea glass, we often become broken in our common life together. Some may even feel that they have been discarded by the world into the depths of the sea. But the promise of scripture is sure: nothing, not brokenness or being thrown away by others will ever separate us from the love of God. Though God is not the author of hardship and trials, God will remain with us in the deep places of the sea, smoothing our hurts and polishing our frailties until our lives take on the beautiful luster and color of sea glass.

In life, we may experience brokenness, but if we trust in God, what we will discover one day is that we have been fashioned into a people who are fully mature, complete, and lacking in nothing. And the beauty people see in us will be Christ's glory; glory that resides in

One who considered every test of life as an occasion for joy.

Remind me, Lord, that in every circumstance I belong to you. Pour through me your strength that I may face every difficulty, trial, and brokenness through your eyes, as opportunities to be fashioned for greater use for your kingdom. Amen.

Pelicans

"When we were utterly helpless, Christ came at just the right time and died for us."
Romans 5:6 (Common English Bible)

Florida has two pelicans, the Brown Pelican who is present year-round and the White Pelican who is a "snowbird" and only arrives in the winter. An exciting bird to watch, the pelican has a very large bill with a rather large pouch used to gather food. Most days they can be seen from the beaches of South Florida diving from great heights, crashing into the water and emerging seconds later with a satisfying meal of fish. I have sat on Delray Beach and counted as many as fourteen flying together along the shoreline overhead. For me, watching pelicans in flight is a most satisfying experience!

The early Christian Church often used images of the pelican as a symbol of caring and self-sacrifice. This was because of a misunderstood practice of pelicans as they cared for their young. While feeding her babies a mother pelican often presses her bill onto her chest in order to fully empty the pouch. The early church thought that the mother was wounding herself - providing her own blood from her chest - when no other food was available. The Dalmatian pelican has a blood-red pouch in early breeding season and this may have contributed to this misperception. As a result, the pelican came to symbolize the death of Jesus that we might have forgiveness and life.

Here in this sentence from Romans, Paul speaks to God's character and achievement, in particular, Jesus sacrificing himself - accepting wounds on his own body - for a people who were utterly helpless because of their sins. Christ's own suffering and death on a cross shows God's gracious, surprising love for us. The careful reader will notice that God's love is not conditional. God doesn't ask anything in return before dying for us. What is abundantly clear is that it was at that point *"we were utterly helpless"* that God did what was necessary for us. For anyone who inquires of the character of God, that is what God is like. God loves us first.

The self-wounding pelican for her young is a legend. More careful observation has taught us much about pelicans. Yet, this legend provides hope, encouragement and strength for me. Each time I am on the beach enjoying a beautiful day I look for pelicans in flight overhead. When I see one - or many - I am reminded of the legend. And that legend is all I need to hear the words again in my heart, *"Christ came at just the right time"* for me.

May every flight of a pelican today remind me of your unconditional love. In the certain name of your Son, my savior, Jesus Christ. Amen.

Hope for a Splintered Church

"All the fullness of deity lives in Christ's body. And you have been filled by him, who is the head of every ruler and authority."
Colossians 2:9, 10 (Common English Bible)

Every serious Christian today, aware of the struggle for building authentic disciples of Jesus in the present generation, must be troubled by the spectacle of a splintered church. Anyone well acquainted with the teaching of Jesus knows that the present divisions of the church are not his will. The prayer of our Lord in John's Gospel is, "that they may all be one – so that the world may believe that you have sent me." The Apostle Paul advances the same in his first letter to the Corinthian Church, "Now I appeal to you, brothers and sisters, by the name of our Lord Jesus Christ, that all of you be in agreement that there be no divisions among you." Divisions simply distract the church from its primary purpose of mobilizing people for the mission of Christ.

The theological divisions of the church are troubling. If we are concerned about this situation, as we ought to be, how is the church to proceed? The Apostle Paul suggests here, in these two sentences, that we seek our separated sisters and brothers not in the valleys of the doctrines that divide but on the mountaintop of a common confession that "All the fullness of deity lives in Christ's body." Affirming with renewed vigor this common confession can heal the theological divides that plague the church. It is living into the conviction that good Christians sometimes disagree but are held together in one confession that Jesus is Lord.

Naturally, this is accomplished when we cease the questioning of our sisters and brothers as to the sincerity of their faith. Such questioning only exacerbates the hurtful divisions. What is better is reclaiming our theological center that professes that the Church in every age needs continual reforming by the spirit of the living Christ. It is being deeply persuaded that there is still more truth to be revealed. From this juncture we may discover that our theological debates, which can often be fierce, can be transformed into a conversation where each of us strives to really hear one another, and hear another point of view.

Faith is not assenting to a set of propositions or following a religious code. Faith is trusting Christ with our lives, as we would trust a friend with our most precious possession. Any hope for a splintered church will not be by abandoning our deepest convictions, nor an apathetic tolerance of another point of view. Rather our hope will be found in a firmer grasp that in Christ, and Christ alone, will our differences be reconciled. As we pursue a deeper intimacy with one another – in the midst of our differences – the church may well arrive at a deeper intimacy with God.

Forgive my arrogance, O Lord. Too often I am convinced that I have grasped the truth and that others are wrong. Rather than building community with others, my differences of thought and belief deepen the divisions of the church. Help me realize again, as the early church professed, that there is still more to know, more to be revealed, and more truth to be understood. In Christ may I seek spiritual communion with others. Amen.

Uneasy Worship

"I know your works. Look! I have set in front of you an open door that no one can shut. You have so little power, and yet you have kept my word and haven't denied my name."
Revelation 3:8 (Common English Bible)

Increasingly today, people go to church when their lives are uneasy and other resources for restoring calm and order have been exhausted. What they seek from church is a healing balm; they look to be soothed with inspirational music and drugged with holy words that promise security. This romanticized notion of church must be confronted with the facts. Church was never intended to be a stable, smug and conventional purveyor of religious sedatives. The prophet Amos corrects this polished impression of God's gathered people, "Doom to those resting comfortably in Zion! (Amos 6:1a)

If the church is called to be uneasy, the Presbyterian Church (USA) is doing something right. There is a deep divide in the present leadership of the church over the Palestinian and Israeli conflict and the question of divesture from companies that are abetting Israeli violation of Palestinians' human rights. The recent Authoritative Interpretation concerning marriage is viewed as not only an act of dishonesty but as unfaithful to the Church's own polity while others celebrate the correction of injustice toward persons marginalized by the church. Absent is the stability and assurance many seek within the walls of our sanctuaries.

The author of Revelation is well acquainted with uneasy worship. Church as an amiable and undisturbed place of comfort is unknown to John. Present is a deep and pervasive uneasiness. It is in the midst of this angst that God speaks a word to John, "Look! I have set in front of you an open door that no one can shut." God's people must now decide. They can withdraw from the present discomfort of the church and seek some physical or mental drug to relieve the distress or accept the challenge to new life and hope; to walk through the open door at the invitation of our Lord.

Acceptance of the Lord's invitation must begin with a new commitment to spiritual formation. If our shared worship and ministry is to be a springboard for a revival of faith and a renewal of the church, we must place our parched lips once more to the springs of spiritual power that flows from a growing relationship with Jesus. It will be the renewal of what the church only occasionally now calls "piety" that will give rise to a new dynamic for engagement in the secular world. The future of the church depends upon the renewal of faith in the living and active Christ and an uneasy worship that recognizes that the kingdoms of this world are in conflict with the Kingdom of our Lord. God sets before the church an open door that welcomes us to a deeper understanding of God's will and a greater reception of God's grace. Moving through that door will demand honestly facing the present uneasiness of the church and the trust that God's Word is true; that what God opens before us can never be shut.

Gracious God, help us to honestly face the uneasiness of the church; to recognize the conflict between our earthly world and your heavenly kingdom, and to choose to walk in the undeniable truth of your word. Amen.

Knowing God's Will

"Trust in the Lord with all your heart; don't rely on your own intelligence. Know him in all your paths, and he will keep your ways straight."
Proverbs 3:5-6 (Common English Bible)

How can we know God's will? It is a real question for many people. The world is so vast, with billions of people on it, that it is occasionally incomprehensible to fathom God takes notice of us much less has a divine purpose for our life. Yet, the faith we encounter in the Bible is that all human affairs are under divine direction – that God has a design for the world and that each one is an integral part of that design. We do not live by chance or fate. Our lives are under the guiding hand of God. Sometimes that guidance is clear and unmistakable. More often, that guidance is reduced to a still, small whisper and listening is difficult. The question remains, how can we know God's will?

Absent dramatic intervention – which was and remains one means God communicates God's guidance – people must develop an eye for the quiet succession of apparently natural events that unfold. Listening is also important. The unexpected impulses, sudden promptings and uncommon challenges that confront us all hold the possibility of God's direction of our steps. Paying attention to everyday situations can awaken us to God's presence and activity in our lives. We shall recognize God in the little things each day – and follow – if we are in touch with God. As exercise strengthens the body and proper diet sustains energy, so the spiritual faculty within us expands through regular prayer and meditation on the Bible.

Immersion in a community of faith is also important. King David listened to Nathan, the disciples honed one another's application of Jesus's teaching and the apostle Paul was instructed in the faith by Ananias. Personal discernment of ordinary events in our lives is important but there are times when it is wise to listen for God's guidance through another. Particularly people who have developed an uncommon capacity to see God in the ordinary, they can enlarge our vision and sharpen our understanding. They see our lives from a different angle and can offer a dispassion take on where God may be actively leading us.

What remains is the hardest – surrendering our lives to God's will. Prayers are more often, "This is what I would like you to do, Lord," rather than, "What would you have me to do?" What we really seek is divine approval of what we desire. The words of Gardner Taylor are wise, "It is hard for us to realize that on this uneven journey there are directions, right choices that we cannot know because we are not God."[4] Perhaps the greatest challenge of the Christian faith is learning that we only have two choices in life – a choice of masters. Either we will remain in charge of our own lives or we surrender ourselves to God and trust in God with all our heart. It is in confidence of the latter that the author of Proverbs wrote.

Awaken my senses, O God, to your presence and activity in my life. Grant that I may discern your claim upon me and understand the direction you call me to go. Amen.

---

[4]Edward L. Taylor, *The Words of Garner Taylor, Volume 2* (Valley Forge: Judson Press, 2000), 24.

When It Is Difficult to Love Yourself

"...and love your neighbor as yourself."
Luke 10:27 (Common English Bible)

Nothing runs deeper in human nature than the desire to be loved. It is seen in people of every age. Children craving attention and approval, teenagers eager to be acceptable and affable to their peers and adults longing to be welcomed and valued. In every age there is present the widespread desire to be liked and loved. There is nothing wrong with this. Approval, acceptance, and appreciation are yearnings of nearly every normal person. Each of us wants to be loved.

It is upon this healthy quality of the human condition that Jesus constructs his Great Commandment, "Love God and love your neighbor as yourself." Yet, for numbers of people there is present a practical difficulty – they have trouble loving themselves. And this is where the Great Commandment comes apart for them. Perhaps because of some physical defect, lack of general attractiveness, or problems with personality or temperament, they have experienced avoidance or blatant rejection. The consequence is pain. Unpopular and unwanted, it is difficult to give to God or neighbor a love they have not known personally.

Desperate for acceptance and community – or simply a friend – lonely people will compromise nearly anything. They will become anyone others want them to be, value what others demand, and behave as others do, even if that behavior is wrong and hurt others. They willingly put to death the person they are. Being authentic only brought loneliness. Peer pressure is the common label used in such circumstances. And it is a powerful weapon by those who would manipulate others to conformity.

Jesus offers an alternative. This very commandment – The Great Commandment – demonstrates Jesus' reverence for people. Jesus assumes that people love themselves because he found them worthy of being loved! This is demonstrated again and again in the ministry of Jesus. Zacchaeus, a tax collector, dishonest and loathed by the people, a woman caught in moral failure, and a man who lived alone in a graveyard, Jesus loved those others ignored. And there is Christ's power. By personal influence he brought out in them what was the finest in them. He gave them a new self-respect and that became the basis of their recovery and transformation. Jesus did this for them. He continues the same today for those who receive him.

Lord, you are the God of peace, mercy, love and compassion. In your goodness, heal the broken places of my heart that I may fully love my neighbor as you love me. Amen.

Holy Speech

"The Lord's blessing makes a person rich, and no trouble is added to it."
Proverbs 10:22 (Common English Bible)

Woven into our common speech today is the language of the church. Perhaps the clearest example - and most often used - is the greeting, "Merry Christmas!" These words roll freely off the lips of all sorts of people at Christmas; merchants at the close of a sale, service providers at the completion of some job, and strangers passing one another on the street. Even Santa Claus is heard using this expression of the Christian Church! The difficulty is that such phrases become depleted of their richness from the causal way in which they are spoken.

Another example is the expression, "The Lord bless you," or more simply, "God bless." This is freely used today, often with little understanding of what is precisely meant. Here is an expression that has passed through the doors of the church into the traffic of secular life. You hear it used tenderly, sincerely, with deep hopefulness or even as a parting word. One television comedian's weekly sign off, "Good night and may God bless" became familiar to his viewers. The question remains for many, what is meant by these words?

Simply, these words, drawn from this passage in Proverbs, mean a benefit, a gift, or a happiness and completeness conferred on us by God. Whether he knew it or not, the comedian who signed-off his weekly variety show with, "God bless" was saying, "I hope God gives to you what is required today for your joy and happiness." What a most pleasant thing to say to another!

Naturally, this is far richer than saying, "Good luck". The words, "God bless" sparkle with a depth and power and meaning that wishing someone, "Good luck" can never accomplish. Perhaps this is because nothing is being left to chance. The phrase, "God bless" preserves God. God is in the words. Though this phrase may have fallen into casual use, the aroma of the faith remains. Next time you use the words, "God bless" understand that what you have done is placed that person into the hands - and heart - of God where untold riches are found and there is no trouble.

Increase in me today, Heavenly Father, the knowledge that you hold me in your grasp and that nothing can separate me from your love. May my speech be generous in claiming this conviction for others. Amen.

Paying Attention to God

*"When you hear of wars and reports of wars, don't be alarmed.
These things must happen, but this isn't the end yet."*
Mark 13:7 (Common English Bible)

Some years ago, I interviewed for the position of senior pastor for a church located in New Jersey. I did not seek out this opportunity; they sought me – receiving my name from someone who thought I would be exactly what they were looking for in a pastor. This search committee had narrowed their search down to one other candidate and me. Grace, my wife, and I were brought to their community for a weekend for further interviews and becoming acquainted with one another. In the Presbyterian Church, this is the typical process for both the search committee and the pastor to discern if the potential relationship is a good fit.

Most of Saturday was given over to additional interviews and showing my wife and me the community. A delightful dinner was catered in the main dining hall of a major corporation headquartered in that state. The following morning – Sunday morning – I preached for the search committee my "trial" sermon. Everything about the weekend felt right for Grace and me and we were prepared to accept their call to me to be their pastor if they offered it. They did not. During lunch with the committee, following worship, they told my wife and me that everything about the weekend felt right to them except one thing they could not overlook. It was this: I preached that morning from a different translation of the Bible than what they preferred. I continue to believe that they choose as their focus that day, the wrong thing.

This is precisely the dynamic of this story from Mark's thirteenth chapter; the disciple's focus is on the "awesome stones and buildings" (Verse 1). Jesus shifts their focus from the present to the future, "Do you see these enormous buildings? Not even one stone will be left upon another. All will be demolished" (Verse 2). The disciples had chosen as their focus that day, the wrong thing. Jesus then announces that evil is expanding – that things were going to get worse - and that all disciples had the responsibility to "watch out;" to be ready for the end. Yet, Jesus tells his disciples. "Don't be alarmed"

(Verse 7). What Jesus declares is that God is still in charge. Rather than becoming pessimistic about what the future holds, followers of Christ are to be optimistic about God.

The end is drawing near. Jesus wants all who hear him to know that we don't have forever. This glimpse into the future is not a call to experience dread and despair. It is a call to focus on living faithfully in the present "just as if" the end will arrive any day. This is not the time to be living without Christ. Nor is it the time to be sloppy in our discipleship as if we have all the time in the world. "Don't be alarmed" when the world looks hopelessly out of control, says Jesus. God alone will determine the end of time. Our responsibility is to pay attention to God in the present, have hope and always be seeking to live faithfully.

Gracious God, open my eyes to see your hand at work in all beauty of the world. Direct my heart, and thoughts, in such a manner that I may live wisely, and obediently in the confidence that my future is held in your grasp. Amen.

Confidence in Christ

"Why are you frightened? Don't you have faith yet?"
Mark 4:40 (Common English Bible)

It is not comfortable to hear the voice of Jesus ask, "Why are you frightened?" Fear belongs to children and the weak. Where fear may be present in our adult lives we conceal it. We are expected to be strong and unflappable; never an easy target for the enemy, whoever or whatever the enemy may be. Yet, here Jesus tears away our pretense, looks directly into our souls and asks, "Why are you frightened?" Nothing – including our fear – is hidden from the Lord.

Is there anyone in the church today who has not known the fear that clutches when divisions arise? The Presbyterian Church USA was once a large force for God in our nation; a proud presence in the local community. By many measures that same church appears reduced to a flickering candle in the high wind of discord within and indifference without. Secretly we agree at times that the effort in which we are presently engaged is a losing battle. How strong, I want to ask in all frankness, how strong really is our faith in God, our confidence in Christ? Jesus presses us, "Don't you have faith yet?"

The spiritual power our churches need today, the spiritual renewal so many of us are seeking is not a diversion from the present strife in the church but right in the midst of it. The faith that develops cloistered from the traffic of our present struggles is not Christian faith. Denial never has produced the strength and vitality that our church hungers for. There cannot be hung an iron curtain between the vigor of council meetings and the formation of individuals into the likeness of Christ. The living faith Jesus calls for, the faith which impels us to meet the present challenges, is shaped in the crux of the challenges, not from escaping them.

The church requires new words and new images to express what confidence in Christ can do for a troubled, conflicted church. Where the body of the church has grown tired and vitality is remembered only in former days, the Gospel hovers around like a ghost whispering, "God still promises life and life abundant." What is required is a crack in the prevailing despair, an opening of hope that once again believes in uncommon possibilities orchestrated by the Holy Spirit. The church needs inward eyes that catches the vision of God's present activity and an inward spirit that responds to the tug of the unseen force of the Spirit and the readiness to let go of the tired religion that may be standing in the way of Christ making all things new.

Father, forgive. Forgive the weariness that fails to believe in new possibilities. Forgive the doubt that hinders faithful obedience. Forgive despair that no longer anticipates your reconciling work. Amen.

The Common Life Lived Uncommonly

"To one he gave five valuable coins, and to another he gave two, and to another he gave one."
Matthew 25:15 (Common English Bible)

It is natural to strive for greatness, for recognition and for making a large contribution. Each one of us is endowed with some talent, some gift and ability and the business of life is to discover what it is. Once discovered, that talent is developed and polished much like a rough, natural diamond that is placed in the hands of a jeweler. No one really wants to be common. Every normal young person has dreams and aspirations and strives to get on with life, to climb the success ladder and pass others in the walk of life.

This is admirable, of course, if the motivation is wholesome and the desire is directed toward worthy ends. But our Lord's parable of the valuable coins is a reminder that there is a limit on each one of us. Some may be endowed with greater ability, but everyone has some limit on capacity for achievement. Five-star generals do not win battles by themselves. Without apology, Jesus teaches that talent and ability is unevenly distributed. Some people will be exceptionally talented and have the potential for greater accomplishment than others. Some are uncommonly gifted and many of us are simply common.

The question then becomes, will we do our best with what we have? Will we focus our efforts for maximum contribution, for the welfare of others or will we begin to whine and recline because we cannot shine? Unreasonable expectations and demands upon us result in chronic unhappiness and diminish not only our lives but also the lives of those who love us. There are far more ordinary doctors, lawyers, persons in the service sector and administrative roles than exceptional ones. Yet, each has the capacity to make an important contribution each day to their families, friends and community.

The simple and practical course to follow is to make a realistic appraisal of our capacity and gifts. This may mean for many the discarding of delusions of grandeur, acknowledging and accepting that in the Lord's distribution of gifts we may have received only one or two talents, and that God's expectation of us is the same as those who received five talents. The acid test of character is whether we have discovered what talent we have and then, having discovered it, placed it to maximum use. That is when the common life is lived uncommonly.

Guide me, O God, to recognize how you have uniquely gifted me for participating in your great work in the world. Then grant me the courage and wisdom to use them in such a manner that lives are impacted with the love of Jesus Christ. Amen.

The Scramble for Success

"An argument broke out among the disciples over which one of them should be regarded as the greatest."
Luke 22:24 (Common English Bible)

Little has changed in the human condition from the day of Jesus' ministry on earth to our day – in every walk of life people seem to be playing the status-seeking game. It is seen in their homes, their furniture, and the car they drive. It is noticed in the clubs they join and the company they keep. Many surround themselves with symbols of their preferred place in the social order. Advertisements advance this endless scramble for position in social rank. Luxury items carefully placed on optimal pages of newspapers and magazines with one aim – promotion of ostentation and snobbery. Success is measured by the stuff we acquire, greatness measured by our position in the company and community.

The unfortunate result of this scramble is that we become self-centered. Everything becomes about us. Even in the church – perhaps particularly in the church – a self-centered nature is revealed in demands that the worship music suit our personal taste, the pastor be more outgoing, and the children be less distracting. Criticism always shows up in someone who is thinking far too much about themselves. There was a case of a woman who made a special donation for flowers in worship one Sunday morning. Mention of her gift was inadvertently omitted from the worship bulletin. Recognition denied, she demanded a refund.

Jesus had a great deal to say about self-centeredness and status seeking. "Watch out for the legal experts. They like to walk around in long robes. They love being greeted with honor in the markets. They long for the places of honor in the synagogues and at banquets" (Luke 20:46). Jesus' remark, "Watch out" could not be clearer. Self-promotion has no place in God's kingdom. For a people who claim to follow Jesus, many of us are missing the mark – some considerably so!

What is a faithful response? First, understand that Jesus never forbade his followers to seek greatness. It is right to seek it, but it must be real greatness. The greatness esteemed by Jesus is one that places initiative, ambition, and developed ability at the service of others; at the service of God's mission. The parable of the valuable coins in Matthew's twenty-fifth chapter is but one supreme teaching of the Bible that God expects us not to be idle. Second, if we are to reverse ourselves in the stream of self-interest and drive for success we must keep before us – morning and evening – the example of Jesus. In him we see love to God as the inspiration of life. There is simply no substitution for the regular reading of scripture and prayer for maintaining our focus on why we live and strive to achieve much.

Father, you alone are eternal. Forgive me for those pursuits which are driven by selfish desires for greatness. Open my eyes once again to the example of Jesus who continually considered the needs of others. Amen.

More of God

*"... that Christ may dwell in your hearts through faith,
as you are being rooted and grounded in love."*
Ephesians 3:17 (NRSV)

Some years ago, a man grabbed me following the worship service and said, "I need more God next year so I'm going to give more money to the church." There was a long line of people behind him wishing to speak with me, so I quickly responded, "Go directly to the Fellowship Hall and have some coffee. I need to speak with you about what you said." His smile indicated that he knew he had disturbed me by his comment.

I have a strong dislike for bad theology – any thought that simply isn't supported by the Bible. The notion that God is more accessible to those who give the greatest dollars to the church is bad theology. There simply wasn't any way I would allow this man's comment to go unchallenged.

When I caught up with him he simply said, "I got you, didn't I?" It was clear that he had baited me, and I took the bait. What he said was bad theology and he knew it. I waited for an explanation.

"Understand," he said, "my greatest treasure in life is my wife and children." He continued that in pursuit of a promotion at work and greater earnings he gave nearly all of himself to his company. In the past year his wife and children saw little of him. At first, they missed him. Eventually they came to accept an absent husband and father. It was this – his family no longer expecting more of him – that unsettled him. "No more." He said. "I'm missing out on what has the greatest value to me."

Then came the explanation I was looking for. He reasoned that if he were to have more of his family he would have to give more of himself to them. "The same is true for God, don't you think, pastor?" He was hungry for God and the past year of grasping for success had made him weary. He needed more God. "I'm going to care more about God this year. God is going to get more of me this year – more prayer, more worship, and more of my financial resources. I'm not missing out anymore." Perhaps this is what the apostle Paul means here in Ephesians by, "being rooted and grounded in love" – and that isn't such bad theology!

Teach me, O God, of the things that have true value and grant me the wisdom to pursue them above all else. Amen.

Ministry of Imagination

"There was a Pharisee named Nicodemus, a Jewish leader. He came to Jesus at night and said to him, 'Rabbi, we know that you are a teacher who has come from God, for no one could do these miraculous signs that you do unless God is with him.'"
John 3:1-2 (Common English Bible)

Nicodemus calls the church to a ministry of imagination. A Pharisee, Nicodemus departs from the narrow, walled-in sectarian views of his colleagues and comes to Jesus in sympathetic inquiry. Perhaps Nicodemus is weary of the wooden, cramping and belittling understanding of the Bible that limits fellowship with others of another point of view. Perhaps Nicodemus fears that barriers of thought and divisions in the fellowship of faith can produce nothing higher than spiritual dwarfs. Perhaps Nicodemus simply wishes for a more expansive and imaginative faith and believes that Jesus can offer the necessary nutriment. For whatever reason, Nicodemus comes to Jesus.

A large faith, a full-grown faith must borrow from others. The genius of maturity is the recognition that a wider vision of this life demands the stimulus of thought found in another's wealth. No one discovers adequate nourishment for their own development within the poverty of self-centeredness and narrow-mindedness. If we are to exercise ourselves in the wider vision of imagination – as does Nicodemus – we must listen sympathetically to understandings not our own. Otherwise we exist only in an echo chamber, our thought never growing, never expanding. It is well documented that even Shakespeare fetched his water of inspiration from the wells of other great thinkers and writers.

J. H. Jowett reflects that one's life, thinking and theology will remain comparatively dormant unless it is breathed upon by the bracing influence of fellowship of thought that is beyond our own.[5] Communion with viewpoints on every side, viewpoints to both the left and right of our own grasp of the Bible and the world of thought, lifts our powers for imagination. It is in a grand and inquisitive imagination that our faith discovers strength and grand proportions.

It is where we acknowledge that Jesus is more than anyone can ever fully grasp.

It would be well if persons of faith were to exercise the same imaginative curiosity of Nicodemus. A sincere recognition of another's position, appreciation for another's point of view and discovery of another's purpose and aim in faith strengthens the fellowship of church. Rather than "leaving the table" when disagreements of faith arise, perhaps it would be a richer and more spacious church if we recall the largest common denominator that has always held the people of faith together, the Lordship of Jesus Christ.

Teach me humility and increase within me the exercise of civility in all my discourse with others. Open my ears, and heart, to hear viewpoints not my own and to value them out of an abundance of love for all people. This I ask, Heavenly Father, in Jesus' name. Amen.

---

[5] J.H. Hewett, *Thirsting for the Springs: Twenty-Six Weeknight Meditations* (London: H.R. Allension, Limited, 1907), 193.

The Secret of Spiritual Power

"But those who hope in the Lord will renew their strength; they will fly up on wings like eagles; they will run and not be tired; they will walk and not be weary."
Isaiah 40:31 (Common English Bible)

A woman stepped into my office today. With tears and considerable emotion, she asked that I pray for the world. She mentioned nothing specific. She didn't need to. Another shooting this week on a college campus that left ten people dead. An accidental bombing of a Doctors Without Borders hospital in Afghanistan killed twenty-two people. Hundreds of thousands of people fleeing terrorism, seeking news homes throughout Europe and the United States. These stories drain our strength and cause us to need renewed power.

In the time that Isaiah wrote these words, his people also faced despair. Threatened by domination by a mighty foreign power, Isaiah's people needed all the encouragement and strength that a genuine faith in God could bring. So do we. Just as the natural rhythm of life demands nourishing food, exercise and rest for the body, the same condition applies to our souls. Spiritual energies are rapidly depleted by the crises, suffering and fear that consume our attention. Replenishing that spiritual energy is urgently needed. So Isaiah reminds his people – and us – that our sufficiency is of God. We remain weak unless we derive strength from God.

How do God's people claim this strength? *"Hope in the Lord,"* writes Isaiah. The "hope" Isaiah speaks of is not wishful thinking or "hoping for the best." Here is Isaiah's call to "trust unfailingly in God." It is a call to "hold onto God" with expectant dependence. A constant reliance on God, meditating on God's words and promises in the Bible, generates spiritual power and makes each of us alert for God's intention to use us mightily for God's redemptive purposes in the world. Isaiah asks that we attach ourselves to God as a child clings to a parent.

As in the day of Isaiah, it still takes time to be holy; to be a people set apart for God's purposes in a world shaken by fear. Schedule time each day for reading the Bible and prayer, for reading devotional literature that awakens the senses to new understandings, and do not neglect moments to simply be still and contemplate God's love. These things, along with weekly worship in a community of faith, gives release to the inflow of God's power that renews strength, restores hope, and lifts hearts as on the wings of eagles.

Father, you guide me with kindness and direct my steps with love. Teach me again that the source of spiritual power is found in daily communion with you, as you are revealed in my reading of the Old and New Testament. Amen.

Overcommitted Lives

"Your servant got busy doing this and that, and the prisoner disappeared."
1 Kings 20:40 (Common English Bible)

Early in my ministry, I served a congregation that had enormous challenges. The former pastor had been removed from ministry, the congregation had suffered a plateau in membership, and the financial health was strained. Much was required to return the ministry of that church back to good health. I poured myself into the mission and ministry of that congregation as the new pastor. I attended every committee meeting, taught a Sunday School class as well as provided most of the preaching and sought to meet all the pastoral care needs of the church. My heart was in the right place; my practice of ministry was seriously flawed. I exhausted myself. The result would be that the quality of my preaching, administrative leadership and pastoral care was diminished. I failed the church from over commitment.

Here is a story in the Old Testament of someone who was asked to do one job well – guarding a prisoner. For a while the man did just that, he stood watch over the prisoner in his charge. He did nothing else. And the prisoner remained a prisoner. Yet, he thought he could do more, that he could "do this and that" to help Israel be victorious in battle. The unfortunate result is that the one thing Israel required of him wasn't done. He permitted himself to be overcommitted and failed.

The character and tempo of modern-day living is captured in my story and the biblical story. We seem always on the move, operating on a tight schedule, all the while an anxious eye on the clock. Rarely are such people trying to demonstrate their worth to others. More often they are simply committed to the mission of their organization and seek to advance it forward. The pace of life grows swifter, the pressure becomes greater and eventually, we discover why God rested on the seventh day after creation. A balance of work and rest sustains us. And any organization is advanced by each of us doing a few things well and equipping others to share in the work.

There are people who are not turning out their best work because they are so "busy doing this and that." A popular expression that is in use today is that they have "too much on their plate." Such people fail to practice discrimination of the important verses the secondary with the ill-fated consequence of doing little well. Perspective is lost and the prisoner – any force that is determined to diminish our work – escapes.

Lord, you created the heavens and the earth in six days and rested on the seventh. Help me learn from your example that life must always be a rhythm of work and rest, of producing and of being renewed as I sit quietly in your presence. Amen.

Motivated by a Vision

"One poor widow came forward and put in two small copper coins worth a penny."
Mark 12:42 (Common English Bible)

Catherine was a woman whose faith moved mountains. A member of a small church I served many years ago, Catherine lived modestly on a meager social security check. The only other financial stream she had come from housesitting people's pets while they traveled. She had little, and nothing about how she dressed and lived suggested otherwise. Yet, to know Catherine was to experience a living parable of God's grace and generosity. Her life was motivated by a vision that neither poverty nor inadequacy could quench. It was a vision that she could be used to change lives.

Each year, that congregation collected food and prepared large gift baskets for under-resourced families in the community. Each basket would have a medium-sized turkey, fresh vegetables, assorted canned foods, and breads and a dessert. Each year, Catherine participated by baking a loaf of bread to be included in one of the baskets. It was all she could afford. It was enough. During my six years of ministry in that church, nearly 100 people told me that Catherine's witness of generosity resulted in their own. My best estimate is that the additional generosity approached $5,000, making those six loaves of bread becomes nearly $5,000 to feed empty stomachs. In my way of seeing the world that is a huge mountain Catherine moved.

Examine this faith. Can yours compare to Catherine's, a faith that drives you to be generous, particularly when you may have little to offer? What sort of faith is this that would make Catherine bake a loaf of bread to feed another family on Thanksgiving? I asked her, and her answer was the best sermon I have ever heard on God's grace. She giggled and said that so many people have a fear of running out. But God's mercies are new every day and so is God's capacity to meet our daily needs. Catherine's loaf of bread was an expression of gratitude. More, she answered, she is part of God's work force helping God keep God's promise to provide for someone else.

This one sentence from Mark's Gospel could be about Catherine. This poor widow trusted in God. The result was a determination - in the face of all evidence to the contrary - to contribute something of significance to advance God's work. Despite the poverty of the offering, she was motivated by a vision. It was a vision that she could be used to make a difference in the life of another. And Jesus noticed.

Heavenly Father, strengthen me by your Spirit and increase my vision for how I may be useful to you and your work in the world. Amen.

Our Compulsion to Complain

"The whole Israelite community complained against Moses and Aaron in the desert. Who are we? Your complaints aren't against us but against the Lord."
Exodus 16:2, 8b (Common English Bible)

"Instead, we are God's accomplishment, created in Christ Jesus to do good things. God planned for these good things to be the way that we live our lives."
Ephesians 2:10 (Common English Bible)

Among my natural gifts is the compulsion to complain. I am not alone. Each church I have served has included similarly endowed people. The compulsion to complain is a very familiar tendency that appears on the stage of life. It may seem to have a relatively small role in the unfolding drama of our life, but it has the capacity to derail the whole play. Complaining can empty our reserves of energy and diminish the ability to see how God may be moving and directing our lives.

Moses had something to say about complaining. Through Moses' obedience to God, he led the people of Israel from the bondage of slavery in Egypt into the wilderness – a journey that would culminate in receiving God's "promised land" that they would call home. But the time in the wilderness would be difficult. Difficulty resulted in complaint. They grumbled that there wasn't enough food. They complained that there wasn't enough water. The days were hot and the nights too cold. After Moses had heard enough he declared, "Your complaints aren't against us but against the Lord." That is because it is God that is calling the people forward into a different future. And sometimes our future requires the preparation of a wilderness.

Because of their complaining their promised future was at risk. Their great vision of freedom and joy was slipping away. More, their memory of slavery was not correctly remembered. They would mumble among themselves how much better it was in Egypt. Nothing was in focus – their future or their past. Now that is insight for a complainer to consider! Complain about the weather if you must. Whine about the rising cost of medical care if you need to vent. But complain about obstacles before you, difficulties and challenges that confront you and problems and sorrows that trouble your heart and Moses tells us that your complaint is against the Lord.

How does one change? Paul's letter to the Ephesians is helpful: change your focus! Rather than dwelling on what is wrong in our world consider how God might use you to better it. We were "created in Christ Jesus to do good things." We were created not to belittle the world with all its difficulties; we were created to better it. Take Paul's word and make it a great experiment for your life. Each morning pledge that you will not complain. Rather, ask how I might make this a better world for others. When you are confronted with personal hurts and difficulties ask, how might I learn and grow from this; how might God be using this to prepare me for a future I cannot now see? Then review yourself at the day's close. How did you do? Obedience to Paul's words here in Ephesians, consistently applied each day, will have the effect of diminishing the compulsion to complain.

Forgive my compulsion to complain, deliver me from selfishness and instill within me a heart of service, for the sake of your holy name, O Lord. Amen.

Willful Submission

"Whoever wants to be first among you will be the slave of all, for the Human One didn't come to be served but rather to serve and to give his life to liberate many people.'
Mark 10:44, 45 (Common English Bible)

Two of Jesus' disciples, James and John, have a favor to ask of their Lord; when he came into his Kingdom they asked for the best seats in the house. Remarkably, there is present no sense of embarrassment. The request is impudent, presumptuous and, undeniably, selfish. Yet, the request is true to human nature as it is revealed throughout every generation. Seeking position, power and recognition is a well-established value that seems hardwired into the human psyche. So here it is seen even among Jesus' disciples – the desire to leverage an opportunity to serve inflated egos and personal ambition. Personal fitness for what they ask isn't a consideration.

This love of power and desire for notice is one of the most insatiable of all human urges. It is also a moral problem that is wrestled with throughout the pages of our Bible. Look at Jesus' response to James and John who jostled to obtain it: "Whoever wants to be first among you will be the slave of all." What a reversal of current standards! For Jesus, no one can be truly great whose life is not viewed in terms of service to another. Our highest self is achieved only through humility and assuming the posture of servant. It is recognizing any position of authority as an opportunity for advancing the common good. What Jesus offers is a life redeemed from pettiness and crudeness.

Naturally, this new understanding of power and position requires some imagination. A world view that shifts from domination by a few over the many must give way to another – one where the world's foundation is spiritual and the knowledge that might is powerless to establish anything that lasts. Ultimately, this is God's world and God settles nothing by might and sheer power. Our destiny is in something deeper and more enduring than power. We see what that is in his cross. Jesus demonstrates that genuine power is one that changes people from the inside out. Love overcomes hate, gentleness depletes the energy of force and people become more responsive to one another, building trust and partnerships.

I do wonder from time to time how the disciples' responded to this teaching. It is not a popular lens to view life nor one most people would want. Jesus is free of pride and arrogance because he recognizes his dependence upon God. And in our best moments we know that if we lived as Jesus – with submission to God – the world would be an infinitely better place.

Direct me, O Lord, in all that I do, and with your favor, diminish the pride and arrogance within me that hinders my growth in Jesus Christ. Amen.

Living with Tension

*"Therefore, stop worrying about tomorrow,
because tomorrow will worry about itself.
Each day has enough trouble of its own."*
Matthew 6:34 (Common English Bible)

A more promising title for this meditation might be: *Living Without Tension*. Yet, that is a promise that is neither realistic nor supported by the Bible. Mark's Gospel declares that on the night of Jesus' arrest, Jesus "began to feel despair and was anxious" (Mark 14:33). Amanda Enayati, writing for *Success* magazine asserts, "The greatest myth is that stress-free living exists at all. In reality the only time you are truly stress-free is when you are dead."[6] Yet, here in Jesus' Sermon on the Mountain, he seems to suggest that we have the capacity to "stop worrying."

Except, Jesus doesn't say that. Jesus teaches that we are to "stop worrying about tomorrow." There is a considerable difference. It is unlikely that any one of us can simply shut-off any concern or worry. What Jesus offers is the possibility of limiting our worry to one day at a time. As Jesus points out, "Each day has enough trouble of its own."

What has been observed over and over again by psychologists is that women and men become tired, run-down and discouraged not by the challenges that confront them today. What drains our energy is our frightened concern over what waits for us on the horizon – what we have to do tomorrow, and the day after that. This doesn't mean that we don't prepare for tomorrow. It simply means that we don't work ourselves up into an anxious knot and fever of apprehension worrying about tomorrow. Today, teaches Jesus, is enough to be concerned about.

What are we to do? All that Jesus had to say about living is fixed firmly on belief and trust in God. God is in our future – we are not left to it alone. The night of Jesus' arrest was filled with tension and worry. But do not fail to notice what Jesus does with it all. Jesus prays. Jesus claims the presence and concern of a living God that restored his energy and brought healing. What Jesus asks is that we do the same. Do our best today and leave the rest to God. This is a truth that we can accept because it comes from Christ. It is first and last the secret of victorious living.

Gracious God, increase my trust in your care and help me live a calm and tranquil life that Christ may be seen in me. Amen.

---

[6]Amanda Enayati, "Dissection Stress." *Success.* December 2015, pages 48-51.

Our Daily Work

"Isn't this the carpenter?"
Mark 6:3 (Common English Bible)

It is an encouragement to recall, that in the days of his flesh, our Lord had a job to go to each day. Daily work was as much a part of the rhythm of life for Jesus as it is for us. Often we permit more impressive accounts of Jesus' life to minimize or eclipse this simple reality – Jesus had to make a living for his family, just as we do. This detail of Jesus' life is not insignificant, and the church is grateful to Mark's Gospel for including it. It is essential for our total view of the Lord's humanity. This knowledge underscores that Jesus entered fully into our humanity and brings him closer to the life of the common person. Additionally, Jesus' work provides a rich perspective for understanding our own daily work.

First, Jesus' occupation as a carpenter brings dignity to all honest toil. In the day of Jesus, any form of manual labor was despised; such occupations were considered the unfortunate lot of slaves. A gentleman or lady would not engage in any activity that would result in soiled hands, or worse, callouses. Deeply embedded in the culture was the conviction that bodily work, particularly hard physical labor, is unworthy of a respectable, free person. Many considered such work degrading. Such was the prevailing culture into which Jesus was born, raised and worked. So, when the question is raised, as it is here in Mark's Gospel, "Isn't this the carpenter?" it is spoken with contempt. It is, as we would say today, an attempt to put Jesus "in his place."

Second, any careful observer of Jesus' life recognizes that the dominant motive behind all that he did was to please his heavenly Father. He declares this himself; "I always do what makes him (God) happy. (John 8:29)" One may feel sure that this same attitude was never absent in the exercise of his vocation as a carpenter. This motive to please God was redemptive – Jesus never found his physical labor distasteful or boring. Rather than dragging himself to the carpenter's shop each morning, Jesus must have arrived to his daily work with enthusiasm. Not because the work was easy or pleasant or even profitable but because by completing a job well, he brought joy to his Father in heaven.

Perhaps, most important, Jesus' work as a carpenter enriched his sympathy and understanding of our common life and prepared him for his redemptive mission. While it is true that for the last three years of his life, Jesus was a professional – a healer, a teacher and equipper for ministry – he worked with his hands for a much longer period of time. He knew what it was to experience hardship and fatigue and to make ends meet on a small income. As a carpenter, Jesus faced many of the same situations and problems similar to those we face. Townspeople sought to diminish Jesus that day by pointing out that he was a carpenter. But their words have become our confidence that Jesus truly did enter fully into our common condition and showed us the way to live with grace and dignity.

Lord, in my own work this day, I ask that you affirm once again the dignity and sacredness of daily toil when it serves the needs of others. Amen.

When Our Spiritual Energies Fail

"But those who hope in the Lord will renew their strength; they will fly up on wings like eagles; they will run and not be tired; they will walk and not be weary."
Isaiah 40:31 (Common English Bible)

These words from Isaiah provide the source of spiritual strength. Every day we need spiritual power to do the will of God and to do it well and with joy. In full view of the challenges that press overseas and here at home, the people of God require all the encouragement, and strength, that genuine faith in God can offer. Today, as in every era since these words were spoken by the prophet Isaiah, these words have brought the people of God both challenge and direction, as well as guidance and strength. And, as each day seemingly becomes more demanding, this source of strength remains equal to the need.

The conviction here is that God's work demands God's power. Just as our physical bodies weaken without sufficient food and rest each day, so do our spiritual energies fail unless they are daily replenished from God. Yet, when Isaiah speaks of, *"hope in the Lord"*, Isaiah is not suggesting that we passively engage in wishful thinking; an optimistic mindset that God will come through for us when the day grows difficult. Rather, Isaiah's use of the word, "hope" is a call to cling our souls to God. "Hope" in the Old Testament is always active, not the passive use that is commonly understood today. It is an expectant dependence on God, a certain confidence that God will renew our strength equal to what we seek.

It takes time to be holy. Yes, we are called to "do good things", as the apostle Paul writes in Ephesians, but always we do so together with God. In our daily time with God, reading the Bible and devotional literature, time in prayer and quiet reflection, our souls receive the inflow of God's power. What a tragic experience it is to witness someone who seeks to do God's will and please God but does not spend the time "clinging to God" in such manner that they receive God's power. In time, their spiritual energies fail, and discouragement overtakes them.

These words close with the promise of unwearied strength. This is not to say that we will never experience physical exhaustion. In the early pages of Genesis, God taught the importance of rest and renewal. God's grand design for our life is a rhythm of work and rest, of producing and being replenished. The promise here is that when our lives are fixed in devotion to God, we may experience physical exhaustion from time to time but always with the exhilaration that God enables us, by faith, to plod forward because we are undergirded by God's grace and enfolded by God's love.

Strengthen me, O God, by the abundance of your grace and power, poured into my life. Encourage me when I am discouraged and lift my eyes to new visions of your continued presence. Amen.

The Cost of Complaining

"The whole Israelite community complained against Moses and Aaron in the desert. Who are we? Your complaints aren't against us but against the Lord."'
Exodus 16:2 (Common English Bible)

Frederick Douglas wrote, "Man's greatness consists in his ability to do and the proper application of his powers to things needful to be done." What Douglas speaks of may be called the claim of positive action – the decision to meet all circumstances not with a negative spirit, but with a positive mind and a useful response. When we meet disruptions in life, little inconveniences and seeming disorder of daily rhythms, it is good to remind ourselves that complaining doesn't improve the situation. What complaining does accomplish is damage – damage to us and to those who must hear our complaints.

This damage is seen in the people of Israel. After leaving their captivity in Egypt, life along their journey through the wilderness becomes difficult. Food is scarce, as is water, and the people complained about the hot days and the cold nights. Their whimpering and complaining eventually became directed against their magnificent leader, Moses, who had faced Pharaoh squarely on their behalf, and secured their release from slavery. Memory of a difficult, even cruel, life in Egypt as slaves faded as they exaggerated the comforts they once enjoyed under Pharaoh. Under the cloud of complaining, their future as a free people grew dim. The great vision of liberty was surrendered to a past not rightly seen.

To this miserable and confused state Moses said, "Your complaints aren't against us but against the Lord." Now that is insight worthy of our best reflection! Often complaints arise from a sense that we have been treated unfairly or a belief that life has been unreasonably difficult. Someone or some circumstance is the blame for a life that is less than what we might have. But tell us that our complaint is against God and we may be forced to consider that God never really promised the ease we feel entitled to. Perhaps, God has placed each of us into a world where there are heavy loads to bear and difficulties that demand our best energies, both mind and body. Some reading this may remember the song lyric of decades ago, "I never promised you a rose garden." God didn't.

Complaining doesn't solve anything. And most agree that complaining is a sign of mental and moral immaturity. Complaining brings nothing of value to the table of life. But complaining does exact a heavy cost. It diminishes a clear view of the presence and activity of God in our lives and it sends friends and acquaintances running – in the opposite direction. What remains is to develop a mental attitude that says, "This is the way things are right now. Where can I see God in this? And what positive response can I make?" It is this new mindset that finally moved Israel out of the desert and into God's promised land.

Protect my heart from complaint and direct my thoughts to your gracious activity in my life that I may not lose the peace you have promised. In Christ's name, I ask. Amen.

Fear at Christmas

"Don't fear, Zion. Don't let your hands fall. The Lord your God is in your midst."
Zephaniah 3:16, 17 (Common English Bible)

Often today you hear Christians express dismay that Christ is frequently left out of Christmas. While that may be true, there is something that is more surprising – there is a noticeable absence of fear during this season. Not the everyday fears we all wrestle with, the fear of spending far more than our resources permit, the fear that holiday guests will misbehave toward one another when they gather and fear what the New Year holds for aging parents. Naturally, these are important, but not the fears that keep popping up in the Bible around the Christmas story. No, the fears that ripple out from the pages of the Bible have to do with what God is up to and what that means for our lives.

The fear spoken of here in this passage from Zephaniah has to do with the fear of being punished. The people had no illusion that they were guilt-free. They had broken promises with one another and with God. Simply, they were not the people God called them to be. So when God suddenly shows up, there is apprehension over God's response. The prophet Zephaniah announces that God has forgiven the people their sins and totally removed their guilt. More, Zephaniah shares a little later in this verse that God comes rejoicing and singing from the depths of God's love for us.

Then there is the fear by nearly every member of the original Christmas cast; the fear that God appearing means a disruption of their lives. Pay attention to the Christmas story in Matthew's Gospel and you see an angel telling Joseph not to be afraid. Read the Christmas story in Luke's Gospel and an angel tells Mary not to be afraid. Later in Luke's Gospel, an angel appears to shepherds and they were terrified. There is fear all over the Christmas story. Where is that fear today during the holiday season?

Seldom is the hardness of the life we have with Jesus frankly acknowledged anymore. Many have conveniently forgotten – or ignored – that the coming of Jesus means that God intends to disrupt our little life plans. Christmas very simply means that we are not on our own anymore to do with our lives as we please. The birth of Christ means that we are called to embark upon a hazardous and straining enterprise, one where absolutely nothing is going to be the same anymore. If this is properly understood, there would be considerably more fear at Christmas throughout the Church. Such fear would demonstrate that the Church really understands what is going on. Perhaps the reason the Church has so few experiences with angels appearing is because there is so little fear.

This Christmas, O Lord, help us to surrender our fears to your care that we may live fully into your purposes for us. In Christ's name, we ask. Amen.

On the Road

"Commit your way to the Lord!"
Psalm 37:5 (Common English Bible)

Perhaps there is no more familiar image in the Bible than the image of the road. We encounter it everywhere. From end to end in the Bible our life is compared to a journey – a journey that is rarely direct or easy. Along any journey circumstances change often requiring a change in how we move toward our destination.

The people of Israel leave their captivity in Egypt and travel toward their own land. But God is concerned that difficulties along the journey will result in the people becoming fearful and turning back, so God leads the people not by the shorter route but in a roundabout way of the Reed Sea desert (Exodus 13:17, 18).

After the magi have honored the new born baby, Jesus, they return to their own country "by another route" having been warned in a dream (Matthew 2:12).

Saul, on the road to Damascus to persecute Christians who are living there, encounters Christ and not only experiences a conversion to the Christian faith but his name is changed to Paul (Acts 9).

Means of travel along the road is different today than in biblical days but what remains the same is the unexpected. Illnesses, loss of a spouse or close friend, career change or any number of unplanned circumstances position themselves along the journey, each demanding a change of course. Life is filled with complexity and progress becomes slow. We are not surprised that Israel might have become discouraged on the road to God's Promised Land. Obstacles along the way can do that.

But pay attention to the "road stories" in the Bible. They are instructive as we begin a new year. Though the pace and direction of these biblical journeys often had to be adjusted according to each unique circumstance, God always remained on the road with God's people. Those who trust in the Lord never travel alone. The ability to adjust to changing circumstances and obstacles is vital to moving forward successfully. But it is committing our way to the Lord and trusting in God that holds us steady until we have arrived at our destination.

Steady me, Heavenly Father, when along the road of life, I meet disappointment, sickness, sorrow or failure. Embrace me in the certain arms of Jesus Christ and direct my steps, this day and all of my tomorrows. Amen.

Distinctive Claims of the Christian Faith

"Pray like this: 'Our Father, who is in heaven,'"
Matthew 6:9 (Common English Bible)

The decline of mainline, Protestant Christianity in America is well documented and reported. Fewer people claim identity as Christians today and fewer numbers occupy seats in worship services on Sunday morning. What seems to be increasing is a notion that no religion is supreme or unique and that each one possess much truth. Tolerance has replaced the missional impulse of the church. While no authentic reading of the Bible supports "intolerance" toward other forms of spirituality or faith traditions, it does advance vigorously the distinctive claims of the Christian faith. Perhaps a renewal of the missional vigor of the church requires a recovery of those claims.

The first of those claims is captured in the first words of The Lord's Prayer: "Our Father, who is in heaven." Those words capture the truth that God is both otherworldly and is knowable, understandable, and lovable. There is a mystery around the periphery of the Christian faith but at its center is a God who seeks to know us and to be known. The first two chapters of Genesis capture beautifully both attributes of God: Chapter one speaks to the mystery of God – a God who by the sheer authority of the spoken word creates and, chapter two, a God who draws near enough to us to fill man and woman's nostrils with God's very own breath.

The second claim of the Christian faith is that in the person of Jesus we see God; that in Jesus we see what God is like. We may know God – though limited – by turning to the person of Jesus Christ. In the life and death and victory over death of Jesus, God is revealed not only in words but in a real person. In the person of Jesus, we witness a God who forgives those that sin, values those pushed to the margins of society and seek the restoration of broken relationships. The Christian faith is not about a formula. It is about a person that desires a relationship with us.

Finally, the Christian faith not only points the way to live, the faith gives witness to a promise that God gives power to those who believe that enables us to live as God desires. Moral insight has little value without moral power. The image that comes to mind is that of a two-person paddle-boat. Alone, our best efforts result only in moving in circles. But with a second person paddling with us, the paddle-boat moves steadily forward. God joins us in that paddle-boat, God's strength working alongside our strength, to move toward that life that satisfies. It is that vital union with God that gives new life. And it is that union that results in a growing love for Christ. A vigorous church will be one that recovers again and again these distinctive claims of the Christian faith.

Pour-out your power upon me, O God, that I may live as you desire and be a witness to your love for all people. Amen.

God Will Guide Us

"Trust in the Lord with all your heart; don't rely on your own intelligence. Know him in all your paths, and he will keep your ways straight."
Proverbs 3:5, 6 (Common English Bible)

The fall semester of my senior year in college would be in England. Arriving at Gatwick Airport in London, I disembarked the flight, entered the airport and immediately experienced considerable confusion. Standing in a common area, bewildered by the signage, I felt a hand on my shoulder: "This is the direction you want to go," spoke a friendly voice. The confusion cleared, my path was made clear, and I was on my way. I am a reasonably intelligent person but that was a moment when I desperately needed guidance.

Anyone honest about his or her own life journey admits moments where guidance is welcomed. It is no mistake that high schools, colleges and universities have "guidance counselors" available to their students. Determining a direction in life is not something to be decided casually. Nor is it a simple matter to discern God's desire and direction for us as individuals. There are simply moments when we are as bewildered as I was when I stood in Gatwick Airport so many years ago.

These words from Proverbs provide help. Rather than be intimidated by the vastness of choices and decisions to be made, Proverbs invites us into a relationship with our creator, a relationship that moves from the mind to the heart. There is a critical difference. The mind alone gathers information, orders data and considers several reasonable alternatives. The entire exercise can be accomplished without ever disturbing the heart from its sleep. On the other hand, try building a relationship with a spouse or friend solely on the arrangement of data. It doesn't work. The heart senses, feels, and longs to know and be known. There is knowledge that is simply unavailable using the mind alone.

How shall we trust and know God with all our heart? We begin by learning of God as God is revealed in the Bible. We continue by doing God's will as best as we understand it from our reading. There is no substitution or short cut. Divine guidance only comes to those who daily seek it in the scriptures. We become sensitive to the nudges and promptings of God until one day we sense a hand on our shoulder and a voice that speaks, "This is the direction you want to go."

Father, send your Holy Spirit to guide my feet that my steps may follow the way of your Son, Jesus Christ. Amen.

A Fresh Approach to Prayer

"Jesus was praying in a certain place. When he finished, one of his disciples said, 'Lord, teach us to pray, just as John taught his disciples.'"
Luke 11:1 (Common English Bible)

In the late 60's and early 70's *The Newlywed Game* was a popular television show. The show would place newly married couples against each other in a series of revealing question rounds that determined how well the spouses knew or did not know each other. There would be two rounds; the wives taken off stage first while the husbands were asked three questions. The wives were then brought back into the studio and asked for their answers to the same three questions. Once the wife gave her answer, the husband revealed the answer he gave – written on a blue card - in her absence. Five points would be awarded to the couple that shared the same answer. The roles were reversed in round two, the wives asked to answer questions about their husbands. The couple that had the highest score at the end of the show won.

Imagine a similar game that put to the test how well we know God, how well we understand God's purpose for our lives. I suspect many of us would be embarrassed. Here, in Luke's Gospel, the disciples came upon Jesus when he was praying. Tremendously moved by what they saw, the disciples asked Jesus to teach them to pray. There is no hint in this passage that the disciples witnessed answers to Jesus' prayers. Results weren't what caught their imagination. There was something else. Something that went much deeper.

If we dispense with the notion that prayer is only about answers, that prayer is simply presenting pleas when we are in need, in danger or a crisis, our eyes are cleared to see what the disciples saw when they came upon Jesus at prayer. In Jesus' prayer the disciples saw a concentration and absorption into a relationship with God of which they had no experience. Jesus' prayers demonstrated a deliberate and sustained cultivation of a relationship with God that would put Jesus in the winner's seat of *The Newlywed Game*. What is clear in this passage is that the disciples wanted the same.

Perhaps the greatest difficulty with prayer today is that many are simply out of touch with God. Prayer is reduced to instinct rather than habit, to approaching God out of need rather than a regular cultivation of a personal relationship with our creator. And that is our deepest need - to renew our acquaintance with God. Prayers that flow from instinct tend to be self-centered. The prayer of Jesus is God-centered. It is prayer that takes time to cultivate and requires extraordinary perseverance. But once this fresh approach to prayer is mastered don't be surprised if another approaches you and asks, "Teach me to pray like that."

Forgive my excuses for neglecting daily prayer. Show me again that deep satisfaction in life is found in a deep, abiding communion with you. In Christ's name, I make this prayer. Amen.

Our Responsibility to One Another

"The Lord said to Cain, 'Where is your brother Abel?'
Cain said, 'I don't know. Am I my brother's guardian?'"
Genesis 4:9 (Common English Bible)

We all recognize this evasive response; perhaps we have used it ourselves: God questions Cain as to the whereabouts of his brother, Abel. Cain responds, "I don't know. Am I my brother's guardian?" When you don't have a good answer, or don't want to answer at all, you are evasive. And many times it works! Even if everyone knows that you are being evasive. Except it doesn't work for Cain, it doesn't work this time. Immediately, God confronts Cain about his behavior; about Cain's anger that results in him killing his brother, Abel. God doesn't let Cain off the hook. Apparently, evasive maneuvers don't work with God.

This story is a reminder that all of us are God's children. It is a story that all of us are connected to one another by our common humanity. We belong to a great family of God that share mutual interests and concerns. Each one should care for all, and all should care for each. This notion of our interdependence with one another is pervasive throughout the Bible. In the twelfth chapter of Genesis, God calls a nation, the nation of Israel, to be a people set apart. The purpose of setting this nation apart is so that God may bless them. And God blesses them specifically so that they may bless the nations of the world. God's concern is always for communities of people. Though God does select particular persons for special tasks – such as Moses and the apostle Paul – they are always selected for the purposes of blessing a community of people.

Naturally, this runs counter to the dominant view of western civilization that values individual initiative, individual success, and personal responsibility. None of that is bad except for when it is used as an excuse for not concerning ourselves with our brothers and sisters who have needs. There seems to be a "survival of the fittest" mentality that suggests that each one is responsible for themselves, and not the responsibility of the community. Where this is most evident is in the distribution of wealth – those who have wealth seem to have little concern about the growing gap between those who have little and those who have more than they need. "Am I my brother's guardian?"

Whether we like it or not, we are. A careful reader of the Bible cannot pretend to miss God's concern for the poor, God's command in the Old Testament to provide debt relief to those burdened by debt and the clear instruction to redistribute wealth in 2 Corinthians 8:14, 15. In fact, as the church gathers for worship, and an offering is collected, the church participates in a redistribution of wealth for "the blessing of the nations." God has established that we have an obligation for the welfare of one another, without which our society disintegrates, and we become fearful of scarcity resulting in selfishness and meanness toward one another. When a child of God dies because they lacked access to adequate health care, or food, or shelter, each of us must be ready. God will ask, "Where is your brother, where is your sister?"

Holy Spirit, open my heart to a rich, abiding love for all people. Pattern my prayer life to include those I know in my prayers, as though they were my brothers and sisters. And give me the courage to love even those I may dislike. Amen.

Living Positively with Our Handicaps

"So I'll gladly spend my time bragging about my weaknesses so that Christ's power can rest on me."
2 Corinthians 12:9b (Common English Bible)

Bragging about our weaknesses is uncommon. What is customary – even encouraged – is that we "hide" our weaknesses and present the illusion of a life that is lived in a tranquil manner that is deep and even and unhindered by frailties. One unfortunate result is the deep disillusionment that is experienced when we find our heroes far too human, with frailties and weaknesses like our own. We look for people who seem to have no limitations, no handicaps, no imperfections and we aspire to be like them. In no small manner, people with weaknesses are not considered worthy of our admiration and praise.

Naturally, the danger of finding such a person, a person who is unencumbered by difficulties and imperfections, is to know someone who also possesses considerable conceit. They need no one; they require nothing for their journey through life, not even God. Worse, when understood correctly, their perfection fails to inspire those of us who struggle with handicaps. Another's perfection can only result in our despair. This is why Paul "brags" about his weaknesses – Paul's interest is that we praise only God and that we find in his broken, imperfect life reason for encouragement as we struggle with our own handicaps.

Paul did pray multiple times that his handicap might be removed. That is a demonstration of his humanity. It is an honest prayer that we have no doubt prayed ourselves. Yet, our spiritual condition is developed, positively or negatively, from the place of our weaknesses. For many, the first and instinctive reaction toward our limitations is a negative attitude – a rebellion or self-pity. We revolt against our limitations. Such a negative struggle often advances to cursing God. What we fail to see is that disappointment with our imperfection arises from conceit – we expect to be perfect. That is a poor spiritual condition indeed!

Paul's positive and hopeful response to his weaknesses demonstrates that anyone, regardless of his limitations, can make a spiritual contribution to the world. History is replete with stories of people who rise up and make great contributions in spite of handicaps. These are the stories that inspire each of us to push through whatever difficulties hinder us and advance our lives and the lives of others. Anyone fortunate enough to have the charm and looks of a prince, excellent physical and mental health and is untroubled by limitations, fails to inspire those who struggle daily under limitations. It is not easy to estimate the spiritual stimulus that comes into human life from handicapped people who have found that Christ's power is sufficient for them.

Remove from me my shame and embarrassment for where I am weak, grant to me the humility to accept help from others and teach me to live each day in gratitude for the gifts and strengths I have. In Christ's name, I pray. Amen.

Jesus in the Everyday

"Jesus and his disciples were also invited to the celebration."
John 2:2 (Common English Bible)

Here is a remarkable miracle, and a remarkable story of Jesus. Remarkable because it places Jesus right in the center of Jewish life, during the celebration of a wedding, when he performs his first miracle – the changing of water into wine. Jesus' first miracle was not healing someone who is sick, casting-out an evil spirit from someone possessed, or raising the dead. Jesus' first miracle was performed in the midst of an ordinary dilemma that seems, in many ways, embarrassingly inconsequential. During a wedding celebration, the host of the party runs out of wine for his guest. That is the dilemma. But, informs the writer of John's Gospel, "Jesus and his disciples were invited to the celebration." And because Jesus was present, he saves the party.

Before Jesus began his ministry, Satan provided several opportunities for Jesus to exercise his divine powers for the extraordinary. When Jesus grew hungry, Satan asked Jesus to simply turn stone into bread and eat. Certainly, Jesus could do that! Jesus refused. Then Satan suggested that Jesus "show-off" by throwing himself off a mountain, to be caught by the arms of angels. Again, Jesus refused. Jesus isn't interested in using his capacity for the miraculous for self-aggrandizement or for his own creature comforts. That would miss the point of why Jesus came to earth. Jesus life's purpose is to live for others.

This miracle announces that there is no moment of life that we ought to get along without God. It goes without saying that the moments of desperation or grief we all experience need God's help. But so do the moments of celebration and joy. This early glimpse of Jesus ministry, his presence at a wedding feast, shows Christ most completely at home in any circumstance and occasion of life. Before Jesus would face the darker side of life, this story vividly reveals a happy Christ who knew how to have a good time. This is a side of Christ that is often overlooked.

Often the church seeks to spiritualize the work of Christ and conclude that he is only in the business of saving souls and renewing lives. The unfortunate consequence is the assumption that Jesus isn't really interested in the commonplace events of life. Yet, this first miracle story announces something quite different. Jesus went to where life was, even ordinary moments, and brought blessings. Jesus is never out of place. This story catches Jesus being interested in everyday living and taking seriously everyday conundrums. Jesus was invited to a wedding celebration and he accepted. And his presence transformed the occasion for everyone.

Lord of all life make me attentive to your presence and power to transform the ordinary into the extraordinary. Never let me forget your desire to be during our lives, in any circumstance and all occasions. Amen.

A Sturdy Faith

"Don't hesitate to be enthusiastic - be on fire in the Spirit as you serve the Lord!"
Romans 12:11 (Common English Bible)

This week I received in the mail a helpful reminder from Jiffy Lube that my car's regular and routine oil change and service was due. The reminder stated, "This isn't just an oil change; it's preventive maintenance to help keep your vehicle running right." Naturally, Jiffy Lube is appealing to my desire that my car continue to meet my transportation needs with little worry. Regular maintenance equals dependability.

This is precisely what the apostle Paul is saying here in Romans. Paul is reminding us that a sturdy faith, a faith that is reliable in every season of life, requires regular and routine maintenance. The difficulty for some people is that they imagine that a Christian faith - and life - can be kept up without any particular effort. As David H. C. Read once shared, "Is your Daddy a Christian?" asked the little boy. "Yes," said his friend, "but he's not been doing much about it recently."[7] What is remarkable in that story is that the poor maintenance of a Christian life can be noticed by a little child!

It is easy to take our Christian faith for granted and rely on being sustained by our past experiences or in the continuing life of our church family. When a reminder card arrives in the mail (or a monthly newsletter from the church!) to attend to our spiritual formation and growth, we simply ignore it. After all, our lives are already full. We simply don't have the time for such a luxury of a daily discipline of reading the Bible or sharing a devotional with another. The sober truth is, like a neglected car, failure to remain enthusiastic in the Christian faith results in a faith that fails us when we depend upon it the most.

You and I are either better Christians than we were a year ago – or worse. The Bible tells us that we simply cannot drift into God's Kingdom. So does our practical experience. We cannot drift into a healthier diet or lifestyle. We cannot drift into a deeper relationship with those we love. And we don't drift into a secure financial retirement. The same is true for our faith. Our Christian faith is confronted daily with doubts and challenges from the ever present evil and suffering around us. Be ready, says Paul. Be on fire in the Spirit as you serve the Lord and your faith will sustain you in the midst of any storm.

Holy Spirit, you are capable of wonders beyond my imagination. Stir within me a fresh wonder of faith and a passionate desire to know Jesus more fully. Amen.

---

[7]David H.C. Read, "Christian Maintenance," *I Am Persuaded* (New York: Charles Scribner's Sons, 1961), 166.

Feeling. Understanding. Believing.

"...the one who draws near to God must believe that he exists..."
Hebrews 11:6 (Common English Bible)

This seems quite simple. How can someone approach a God who has no real belief that God exists? Would anyone think of coming to God unless they first thought there was such a being? Why would Hebrews make such an obvious observation? Yet, even the most faithful among us confess to moments of uncertainty. Odd, isn't it? There are moments in life when the existence of God seems highly unlikely. Yet, even in the midst of doubt and uncertainty, there are people who pursue God.

Henry Sloane Coffin offers help.[8] He suggests that we pay closer examination to precisely what claim Hebrews is making. The author of Hebrews does not say, "The one who draws near to God must 'feel' that he exists." Each of us has those moments when we feel the presence of another in the room, even if the room is dark and the other person cannot be seen. But such feelings fluctuate and can be unreliable. They are not always accurate. Sometimes that feeling of the presence of another is only our imagination. Couldn't the same be true for feeling the presence of God - our imagination?

Nor does the author say, "The one who draws near to God must 'understand' what he is." Few reach God with their minds. Any search for truth only results in the discovery of fragments of truth, often unrelated to one another. Any one of us may desire to explore the unknown with reasonable thought but often the result is that God becomes unreal to us. Let us not make the mistake of trying first to understand before we begin our exploration. As Coffin puts it so clearly, we must first touch the shore and land before we can explore the continent and chart out the mountains and rivers and plains.[9]

What does the author say? He writes, "the one who draws near to God must 'believe' that he exists." The question is one of belief. And this chapter begins with the author's definition of belief; giving substance to that which is hoped for. Belief in God begins with "hope" that there is God and then continues by rearranging one's whole life in a manner to live as if that hope is sure. This is what

Hebrews means by 'giving substance' to our hopes. Whereas the reasonable person often begins with evidence first, followed by belief, Hebrews contends that living as if something is true - believing that God exists - produces the evidence. Living the promises of God before there is any proof that they can be trusted is what draws us near to God.

I ask that the counsel of your word, the Bible, direct my steps today that in living into your promises I may discover their power for my life and know that you are God. Amen.

---

[8]Henry Sloane Coffin, "Religious Prepossessions," **University Sermons**. (New Haven: Yale University Press, 1914) 19-35.
[9]Coffin, pages 24, 25.

Why Go to Church?

*"Jesus went to Nazareth, where he had been raised.
On the Sabbath he went to the synagogue as he normally
did and stood up to read."*
Luke 4:16 (Common English Bible)

People are leaving the church – one major study indicates that people are scrambling for the exit doors of the church. Those who remain are becoming less frequent in worship. The felt need for a personal faith is undiminished. Religious convictions remain strong in our nation according to the same study. And many strive to live in a manner that is in accordance with those convictions. The difficulty is that people are becoming impatient with the church as an institution.

Luke's Gospel records of Jesus, "On the Sabbath he went to the synagogue as he normally did." This observation is made as a sidebar in a larger narrative, but it is noteworthy. What it tells us is that the personal habits of Jesus included as a priority the regular participation in corporate worship. Naturally, Jesus knew, as any of us that God can be worshipped anywhere. He could have found support in his day that holy moments can be realized in quiet meditation and private prayer, under the open sky. In fact, each of the four Gospels record Jesus doing just that – moments of prayer in a garden, upon a mountain and – agonizingly – upon a cross. Each place made sacred by prayer and personal worship. Nonetheless, on the day of the week when the faith community gathered for public worship, Jesus was present.

Close attention to the Gospel stories offers nuanced clues that much of the preaching Jesus heard was boring and the worship uninspiring. Yet, the fact of the matter is that the character of the worship services did not affect his attendance. For Jesus, the house of God was a spiritual home. It was where the people of God belonged. Participation in shared worship offered a reminder that life is lived for something larger and finer and more enduring than a preoccupation of the individual life. As Theodore Roosevelt once wrote to his wife, "I feel that as much as I enjoy loafing, there is something higher for which to live."[10]

Yet, right at the end of this brief verse in Luke's Gospel lay the most compelling answer for the question, "Why go to church?" Jesus stood up to read. Corporate worship provides the opportunity of contribution, as well as the receiving of religious experience. A shared witness and a mutual encouragement in our faith journey are simply absent in private moments of worship and prayer. The church may struggle with tedium and uninspired worship from time to time. But worship is not about us – and our needs – as much as it is about the community of God's people and how we might be used to strengthen one another.

Remind me that true worship is not about me, O Lord. Open my heart to claim my responsibility to corporate worship that I may be an encouragement to others and publicly praise your name. Amen.

---

[10]David McCullough, **Mornings on Horseback** (New York: Simon & Schuster, 2001), 30.

Eyes of Faith

They asked, "Isn't this Jesus, Joseph's son, whose mother and father we know?" How can he now say, 'I have come down from heaven'?"
John 6:42 (Common English Bible)

It rarely occurs to us that the ordinary can be a door through which heaven opens to earth. If something comes from heaven it must come in an unusual way, through some mysterious and unfamiliar channel. Heaven and earth are not usually viewed as being in communication. Certainly, the Old Testament does witness to God's use of prophets to speak. But ordinarily heaven and earth stand quite apart. God and humanity live two distinct and different lives.

This was the thinking that caused some to question the authority of Jesus, "Isn't this Jesus, Joseph's son, whose mother and father we know?" How can he now say, 'I have come down from heaven'?" This is "Bible-speak" for ordinary; Jesus was born to ordinary people just as we all were. Yet, Jesus declares he has come down from heaven. It simply doesn't follow that the familiar can be heavenly, the ordinary the activity of the divine. And it is this thinking today that diminishes our own expectation of the sacred in the midst of our ordinary lives. We do not expect a divine encounter in our ordinary existence.

Jesus believed that heaven and earth were in constant communication. God is always in touch and intervening in the lives of God's children. What is necessary for us are eyes of faith, eyes that see the portals of heaven open wide and that God is continually coming into our ordinary lives, transforming them into the extraordinary. Jesus says as much when he responds to Peter's declaration of Jesus' Lordship that this confession of faith was not Peter's only, but God's witness through him, "no human has shown this to you. Rather my Father who is in heaven has shown you." (Matthew 16:17)

Here, in this passage, we are invited to look once more for the possibility of the sacred in the ordinariness of life. Familiarity, if it doesn't breed contempt, at least removes the surprise. If we can account for something we at once conclude that God has nothing to do with it. God is kept as a last resort for events otherwise inexplicable. Yet, here in John's Gospel, we are reminded that through the common life of Joseph and Mary, God did break forth into the world.

Grant me the eyes of faith, O God, to see your extraordinary work in the ordinary rhythms of today. Amen.

Overcoming Defeat

"Then a heavenly angel appeared to him and strengthened him."
Luke 22:43 (Common English Bible)

Three weeks ago, our daughter, Rachael, caught a flight from Fort Lauderdale International to Vancouver, British Columbia to begin her new career as a professional photographer aboard the Volendam, Holland America Cruise Lines. Naturally, she was a bundle of energy, a mixture of excitement for the opportunity and concern for whether she had prepared sufficiently for the journey. She had made an eight-month commitment to Holland America which meant she would be away from our home for that length of time. A crucial question was if she had packed all she would need for that time away.

The question of adequate preparation, of securing adequate resources for a journey touches each one of us. The closer we move to the time of departure that question can become overwhelming. Have we enough for both what we anticipate and for what we cannot see? Will we have all that we need to triumph over all unforeseen challenges? It is well for any of us to experience some measure of anxiety about these questions. Only the foolish begin a journey without thought of what may be required.

An equally important question is do we have the spiritual resources to conquer what is inevitable to us all, moments of discouragement, disillusionment and exhaustion? How will any of us keep the fire of a true devotion to God burning when life thrust us into a crisis? Descending upon us like a sudden tornado, our sheltered and comfortable life can be swept away in a moment by rough winds. With a life now wrecked and in a ruined heap the enemy of defeat lingers near, ready in a moment to destroy us. Defeat is a worthy adversary. Is our faith sufficient for the strain?

That day comes to all of us, the day when we experience a desolating sense of human weakness and an inadequacy sweeps over us. It is a day when the road becomes steeper and the journey lonelier than any of us could have ever imagined. It is precisely on this day that we must remember that as followers of Jesus we have more than our natural resources; that there is more available to us than what we packed for the journey. In that testing hour we have a supernatural resource, an outer power that is as sturdy as an oak and as intense as the sun. For Jesus that power was received from a heavenly angel. For us that strengthening angel may be some shining truth from the Bible, an encouraging word from a friend or a quiet strength received from time in prayer. The angel that comes appears differently to each of God's children. But the angel does come. We need only to keep our eyes – and hearts – wide open that we not miss it.

Father, rescue me from a despair that anticipates nothing from you. Open my eyes and tune my ears to the rustling of your presence and strength in my time of discouragement and weakness. In Christ's name, I ask. Amen.

Filled by Christ

*"All the fullness of deity lives in Christ's body.
And you have been filled by him, who is the head of every ruler and authority."*
Colossians 2:9, 10 (Common English Bible)

This simple truth, that we have been filled by Christ, directly impacts the nature of our Christian life. Guidance for our decisions, the pattern of our behavior and inspiration for the common tasks of life each comes from our communion with Christ. This is what the New Testament means by, "walking by the Spirit" – the glad and spontaneous response to the love of the risen and living Christ. Jesus desires to have the same quality of relationship with us as does a good friend. The best of friendships are those that gently but courageously work in the depths of our hearts to change our habits and shape us to be better. It is this influence upon us that Christ seeks.

Unfortunately, there are some people of faith that never understand this. Their faith is one lived according to the law – a code of religious or moral duties which are accepted as binding. With a clear set of rules in hand, such people strive to please God by sheer effort of self-discipline and restraint. They seek to "get it right" by their own strength, convinced that this is what God wants in a relationship with us. What's more, they do their best to impose their rules upon others. No one really wants to suffer alone.

Naturally, there is nothing wrong with living a disciplined life. The exercise of faithful obedience to the teachings of our Lord is an important part of following Jesus provided such a decision is freely accepted and not imposed upon others. But we must never substitute faithful obedience for a loving, grateful and direct relationship with the person of Jesus. God's call to us has always been one to a relationship with God's Son, not a rulebook.

With our primary attention directed to building a relationship with Jesus rather than learning the particulars of a rulebook, life is filled with wonder and mystery and delight. The joy of discovery that is characteristic of any relationship always trumps the experience of being observed by a watchful eye ready to pounce when we stumble.

As our relationship with Jesus grows, life is lived with the confidence that one day we will be complete, not because of anything we have accomplished but because of what God has promised to accomplish in those who love him.

Increase in me, O God, an awareness of your presence in my life and my desire to know and love you more fully. Amen.

Faith in Prayer

"Jesus was telling them a parable about their need to pray continuously and not to be discouraged."
Luke 18:1 (Common English Bible)

I believe in prayer. I believe that prayer is the most important fact in the life of anyone who determines to follow Jesus. The trouble with prayer is not belief in the practice – it is what is expected from the practice. For many, prayer is practiced as some sort of holy magic. Pray correctly and with enough faith and the desired result arrives every time. Unanswered prayer is simply the result of praying incorrectly or with insufficient faith. This belief is troubling if not downright harmful to a person of faith. In this sentence from Luke's Gospel, Jesus teaches that we are to "pray continuously." Rather than suggesting yet another formula for prayer – pray continuously - I believe our Lord is inviting us to discover at least two ways that prayer is effective.

On one level, prayer opens the one who is praying to a relationship with God. Meaningful relationships are not built by one or two sentences that are shaped into a request, not with God or anyone else. "Continuous prayer" is the cultivation of a regular conversation with God. This is the kind of conversation found naturally between two people who care for one another. Whether we are angry or thankful, whether we are sharing from a broken heart or celebrating, we share continuously with those whom we love. Such conversations draw us closer to one another. It is that closeness with us that God desires.

A second level involves the one for whom we pray. By our prayers that person is not alone. Continuous prayer keeps them in the fellowship of our thoughts and in our hearts. A community of faith is created which liberates them from walking a difficult path unaccompanied by someone who cares. Encouragement and strength bubbles forth when we know that there is someone who is "pulling for us." Creating community among people of faith is one result of continuous prayer.

Faith in prayer does not exclude expectations of the miraculous. God is still in the miracle business. But we are guilty of a grievous error when we reduce prayer to "getting what we want." That makes God a dispenser of religious goods and services while we continue to build the life we want apart from God's claim upon us. Christian prayer is always undergirded by a conviction that God is reconciling us to God's self for the purposes of being used by God for God's ongoing work in the world. "Continuous prayer" is an affirmation that our life is not ours to do as we wish. We belong to God and it is for God that we live.

Lord, enlighten the eyes of my mind to understand that the greatest gift of prayer is communion with you. Amen.

Our Sacred Work

"Learn from me."
Portion of Matthew 11:29 (Common English Bible)

I never imagined that I would have the opportunity to travel to the Holy Land. Colleagues in ministry have spoken of how this holy pilgrimage changed their life in deeply profound ways. I accepted their words as sincere. Yet I had no capacity to understand. Such a trip seemed out of reach for me. Now, through the gracious and generous gift of one family in this congregation, my wife, Grace and I have returned from Israel. In the span of eight days we followed the way of our Lord along the shore of Galilee, the Mount of Beatitudes, entered the gates of Old Jerusalem and walked the Via Dolorosa – the path taken by Jesus with a cross on his back. The impact of that experience is still emerging. I anticipate it will continue to present surprises – in thought and emotion – for some time.

There are two impressions, in particular that have pressed against my heart from this sacred pilgrimage: the sense of memory that remains in locations known to our Lord, and the recognition that the Lord has moved on. Both bear the capacity to impress a deeper reflection upon personal discipleship; the personal quest to acquire the Lord's thought, to carry on the Lord's spirit, to participate in the Lord's vision of a new world and to embody that vision in our own lives. The abundant wealth of such a robust discipleship requires attention to three words of our Lord, *"Learn from me."*

Today, people of many different nations make the journey to Israel for just this purpose, to learn more of Jesus. Though motives for the journey may be expressed differently, all come because of a basic curiosity. And curiosity is always the pursuit of information, of deeper understanding. They have come to learn of Jesus, to learn from him. Someone once remarked that the secret of learning is to ask much, to remember much and to teach much. This provides a helpful pathway for our own discipleship. It is a fruitful approach to successful learning in the school of Jesus.

Each disciple of Jesus must devise their own curriculum to learn from Jesus. But let no one assume that they are alone in the labor of learning. Standing in a footprint of Jesus along the shore of Galilee or walking along the way of the cross may stir remembrances of our Lord and inspire the heart to know more of him, but none of us are alone in this labor to be students of Jesus. The absence of Jesus embodied in flesh at each sacred location reminds us that he has now come in spirit as a great helper in the sacred work of discipleship. That, perhaps, is one of the glories of the ministry of Jesus Christ. While we seek to learn of Jesus, he is at work within us in such a manner that the beauty of the Lord grows upon our vision.

Heavenly Father, as I live each day, help me to remember to learn from you. Amen.

Authentic Friendships

"So Jonathan again made a pledge to David because he cared about David as much as he cared about himself."
1 Samuel 20:17 (Common English Bible)

There is a great reversal of values in this brief passage – a reversal of how the world generally approaches friendships. The message we generally hear from childhood is that friendships can be an opportunity to advance oneself. Make the right friends and you will be positioned for good opportunities. Friendships made less wisely may become meaningful but will do nothing for personal and professional development. The evidence of this may be found in the common axiom, "It's not what you know but who you know."

In this one sentence of scripture we hear something completely different. Jonathan once again affirms his friendship to David simply because he cared about David. Absent is any hint that the friendship is about something else; about using the friendship for personal advantage. Jonathan loved David, cared deeply about David. That was enough reason for pledging his continued friendship. That seems to me to be a better reason for pledging a friendship to another – simply because there is something about another that you love.

What I have found true is that there is a benefit of friendships chosen wisely. The benefit I speak of is that good friends tend to make me a better person. They demonstrate to me how to care more deeply and live for something larger than myself. There are some whose support and love for me makes me a better pastor. And I am deeply grateful for all of this. Yet, I keep coming back to this sentence of scripture. Jonathan again pledged friendship to David simply because he cared about David as much as he cared about himself. This seems to me to be a richer foundation for building friendships than looking for personal opportunity.

So what are we to do? What does this sentence from the Bible say to us? Perhaps, more than anything else, what God desires that we hear is that we should think of ourselves a little less throughout the day. Take time each day and put aside personal goals and aspirations. Put aside any thought of personal hurts and disappointments. Put aside anything at all that has to do with oneself and simply love someone else. Who in your network of relationships simply needs your love right now? If you would quietly, in your heart, pledge once again to love them without any thought of returned value, you will discover something about how God works. You will discover your own life richly blessed.

Forgive me, Father, for thinking more about my life and less about others. Help me today to simply love and value someone else as you love them. Show me clearly how to do this. In Christ's name, I ask. Amen.

Complete in Christ

"All the fullness of deity lives in Christ's body. And you have been filled by him, who is the head of every ruler and authority."
Colossians 2:9, 10 (Common English Bible)

John Leith, author and teacher of Reformed Theology, once commented to me that the single greatest threat to the church is amnesia – the church forgetting that she is complete in Christ. That comment was made to me nearly thirty years ago! With clarity and uncommon wisdom, Leith removed the clutter of the thousand reasons given for the decline of the church in the United States. Since his death, the church has continued on its downward trajectory, both in membership and worship attendance. If we are concerned about this current state of the church, as we ought to be, what should we be doing about it?

The apostle Paul offers insight in these few sentences: *"And you have been filled by him."* Any vessel, any person, any heart that "is full" lacks for nothing; it is full. Paul teaches here that we have been filled with Christ – that Christ alone is sufficient for all our needs. Nothing more needs to be added. Every book in the New Testament announces this truth yet the church today often fails to offer it with authority and in a compelling manner. When people, whose emotional resources have been depleted, approach the church, it seems rare that the individual is directed to Christ and Christ alone. Physical needs may be addressed – which Jesus affirms is important – but asking them to lean into the arms of Christ is absent.

Once this truth is reclaimed – that we need nothing more than Christ to satisfy a heart that is desperate – it follows that we will draw our inspiration for daily life from his life. Guidance for our decisions, the pattern for our behavior and the manner in which we love one another will flow organically from our communion with Christ. As Christ continues to occupy our thoughts and heart, we become agents by which Christ's continued presence and ministry is experienced in the world. Christ changes us as good mentors change for the positive those under their supervision.

What does this lesson from Paul mean for the church? What is primary, I believe, is that the church cannot offer what it lacks. I speak of a deep conviction that the testimony of the Bible is sure; that Christ can be trusted and with that trust comes spiritual power that is palpable. We begin with ourselves. We begin to fully recognize once again the Kingship of Christ who is the Head of the Church, to read the Bible and actually do what we are instructed to do – to live as we understand Christ calling us to live. One life changed is infectious. It can change the church.

Pattern my life in the manner of Christ, fill me with your Spirit and guide me to return good for any evil done to me that Christ may be seen in me. Amen.

Christianity and Communism

"The Spirit of the Lord is upon me, because the Lord has anointed me. He has sent me to preach good news to the poor, to proclaim release to the prisoners and recovery of sight to the blind, to liberate the oppressed, and to proclaim the year of the Lord's favor."
Luke 4:18 (Common English Bible)

Raised in the sixties and seventies, I was taught to loathe and fear Communism. I was taught well, and I did. Yet, as childhood gave way to adulthood my capacity to think and reason for myself developed. One natural result was that I began to question everything, including the political ideology of Communism. College studies introduced me to *The Communist Manifesto* and my curiosity continued to mature and deepen. My knowledge of and appreciation for the Bible also matured. Imagine my surprise to discover that both books shared a core value: a passionate concern for the poor and social justice. According to Luke's Gospel, Jesus' first recorded sermon establishes this value as intrinsic to his mission and ministry.

This uncomfortable truth is why many Protestant pastors supported Fidel Castro's revolution in Cuba and his establishment of a Communist government. The great social needs of the Cuban people, once the responsibility of the Christian Church, would now be addressed more comprehensively by the government. The hungry would now be fed, the naked clothed and the poor provided opportunity. This all had the familiar sound of the Bible. The question pressed, what exactly is there to loathe and fear about that? Christianity and Communism shared the same ideals.

Yet, there is a critical difference between Christianity and Communism – a difference that became very much apparent during my recent invitation to preach in Havana, Cuba: Communism makes no place for God. Communism expects to usher in a new day of equality for all people by its own, unaided efforts. Faith is held in low esteem, as having little or no value. A Communist government acts with purpose. Christianity cedes responsibility to an unseen deity. Naturally, this is the position of the Communist government. The primary difficulty arises when the government seeks to advance its values through any means including force, violence, and imprisonment. The same people the government seeks to help are treated as instruments for the Communist cause.

I no longer loathe and fear Communism – those are strong words. Nor do I entertain any notion that Communism is the hope of the world. The world has one hope, and that hope is centered in the person of Jesus Christ. Under Communism, life is cheap. In the Christian faith, each person is valued as one created in the image of God. Communism advances its ideology through force and intimidation. Christ advances his mission through the transformation of the human heart. Cuba lacks that perfect society for which The Communist Manifesto aspires. That is because such a society is formed only by people whose hearts that have been changed by love.

Lord, I thank you for the great power of the risen Christ. Remind me that only in the person of Christ can lives be transformed and the world changed for the common good. Amen.

Doubt and Faith

"Will my Lord reject me forever? Will he never be pleased again? Has his faithful love come to a complete end? Is his promise over for future generations? You are the God who works wonders; you have demonstrated your strength among all peoples."
Psalm 77:7,8,14 (Common English Bible)

British singer, Adele, has struck a deep place in the hearts of millions with her single, "Hello", a piano ballad. The lyrics discuss themes of nostalgia and regret and it is the first song in history to sell over a million digital copies in a week. Lyrically, the song plays out like a phone conversation, "Hello, it's me. I was wondering if after all these years you'd like to meet, to go over everything." The difficulty is, the person to whom she places the call never answers, "I must have called a thousand times. But when I call, you seem never to be home." Certainly, these words resonate with different listeners in different ways. For me, they express my prayer life some days. I place a call to God, but God never answers. "Will my Lord reject me forever?"

People of faith occasionally experience conflict in their relationship with God. There are moments when it seems easy to affirm God, to believe in a larger purpose than our own small lives, and that, in Christ, we are called to participate in a high and holy purpose. Other moments, faith is questioned. These few verses from Psalm 77 speak of both, of faith and doubt. It is a conflict that is familiar to many.

What are we to do? Herbert H. Farmer proposes an extremely important question, "To which of these two voices in the soul concerning God are we going to make up our minds deliberately and consciously always to give the greater weight?"[11] Will we place faith on trial, demanding evidence before trusting in God? Or, will we place doubt on trial, demanding that it answer the evidence of God's work in our lives? Unless we are deliberate with our answer, we will continually oscillate between the two, between faith and doubt, with the circumstances of life driving the condition of the heart.

It seems reasonable to me that the better choice is not to leave such an important matter to the uncertainties of life. I have experienced moments of doubt and I am certain I will again. Yet, I have made the deliberate decision to place my doubt on trial in every instance. Like the author of these words from Psalm 77, I have chosen to answer every moment of doubt with the evidence of God's marvelous work of wonders, with every demonstration of God's strength among those who know and love him.

God of mercy, replace moments of doubt with the memory of your faithfulness in the past and confidence of your continuing love. Amen.

---

[11]Herbert H. Farmer, "Doubt and Faith," **Best Sermons: 1947 Edition**, edited by G. Paul Butler (New York and London: Harper & Brothers Publishers, 1947), 146.

Isn't It Enough to Be Decent?

"God's goal is for us to become mature adults – to be fully grown, measured by the standard of the fullness of Christ."
Ephesians 4:13b (Common English Bible)

My daughter, Rachael has recently received a promotion from Holland America Cruise Lines. After eight weeks as a ship photographer, Rachael was selected to receive special training by world-renown portrait photographer, Joe Craig, for Black Label Studio work. No longer will Rachael walk the common spaces of the ship, photographing the guests of the cruise line. She will now occupy a studio aboard the ship and accept appointments. More importantly, the standard of excellence for her photography has been significantly raised. Her work will be measured by the standard of Joe Craig who has spent a career building his product image.

The cost of her work has also risen – as much as four times the cost of the product she originally created for Holland America guests. A quick glance at passengers' reviews online shows wide dissatisfaction with the increased price structure. Yet, for every critical review – every single one at my review of posted comments – surprise and delight is expressed at the unusually high quality of the product. "Outstanding," "We were smitten" and "Far and away better than anything I have seen before" are customary comments.

In matters of faith, many today are asking the question, "Isn't it enough to be decent?" Increasingly, people have little interest in the Bible, the church or worship. They declare that "right" behavior is what really matters. One difficulty with this argument is that the standard for this "right" behavior isn't identified. More, few are prepared to acknowledge that their vague sense of what is "right" draws heavily upon inherited spiritual capital. They never wrestle with the question, "How long will decency last if the Christian faith continues to decline?"

The larger question is, "What pulls us forward in this life?" Do we settle for the common photograph available for a modest price or will our standard be higher? We all strive for something. Here, in Ephesians, we learn that God's desire is that our standard for moral behavior and values be nothing less than the standard of Christ. In photography parlance, God invites us to nothing less than a Black Label Studio portrait for our life. Isn't it enough to be decent? No, it is not enough. And the practice of our faith is what will take us into God's studio. The result will be a life "far and away better than anyone could have imagined."

Father, the source of all encouragement, give me the strength to act as one called by you, the conviction to speak as one who has experienced your power and the wisdom to practice all that I have learned from sacred scripture. Amen.

The Responsible Exercise of Faith

"Then Jesus went into the temple and threw out all those who were selling and buying there. He pushed over the tables used for currency exchange and the chairs of those who sold doves. He said to them, 'It's written, my house will be called a house of prayer. But you've made it a hideout for crooks.'"
Matthew 21:12-13 (Common English Bible)

Recently, a presidential candidate was critical of the pope's comments on climate change. The candidate asserts that science should be left in the hands of scientists and that the pope should focus on theology and morality. What is comical about his remarks is that, as a Roman Catholic himself, he fails to grasp that caring for creation and climate change is within the realm of theology and morality. The Christian tradition is built upon God's first vocation for us to be gardeners that protect, care for and sustain God's good creation.

Certainly, there isn't consensus on the topic of climate change nor do I pretend to resolve that issue here. What is clear from this scripture from Matthew's Gospel is that nothing is outside of the realm of God's concern – climate change, business and economics, and personal morality – and that the church is called to speak on every issue that impacts God's creation and how we treat one another. It simply cannot be ignored that in this passage, Jesus "concerns himself" with business and commerce.

There is no getting away with the fact that much of what harms our earth and creates economic disparity among people is permitted because God's people have never placed the inequity of it all on their conscience. It is fashionable to be tolerant, some may say. While many would agree that tolerance is a virtue it should never be confused with apathy or indifference, which is vice. There are evils in this world that demand for God's people to speak, "These things should not be!"

The responsible exercise of the Christian faith calls for men and women to make it their business to care for God's earth and to create a community where people experience a political and economic climate that is humane and just, sound and wholesome. Because people differ on how that might be done – thus different political parties – our behavior toward one another must be exercised with civility and humility. Nonetheless, the world that God intends requires people who are sensitive in conscience, discerning of God's movement and militant in action.

Lord Jesus Christ, deepen my concern for others and love for creation. Show me how to be a responsible steward of everything lovingly created by God. Amen.

Life's Disappointments

"I have shown it to you with your own eyes; however, you will not cross over into it."
Deuteronomy 34:4 (Common English Bible)

This is a remarkable picture of Moses! He is at the point of death, on a mountaintop, gazing out over the Promised Land, a land for which he led God's people to possess, pondering God's Word to him that he himself will never enter the land. A universal truth of life is captured in this tragic moment, a truth that neither the great or small among us escapes; life brings equal capacity to experience joy as well as disappointment. This singular moment of Moses' life lays hold of our imagination as no other moment in his life does. Life sometimes falls short of what is desired and for which we intended our labors to provide.

That moment is on the horizon for every one of us – that moment when we realize that our grandest dreams and the greatest desires of our heart may not be realized. Moses wanted to cross over into God's Promised Land and the apostle Paul urgently wanted to take the gospel to Bithynia. Both were denied. Both their circumstances and own earnest efforts gave Moses and Paul every reason to believe their central purpose and passion in life would be achieved. But what would lie beyond their vision was the disheartening experience of watching their dreams tumble to the ground. "I have shown it to you with your own eyes; however, you will not cross over into it."

What are we to make of this? We do not have access to Moses' inner thoughts as he sat upon that mountain, looking out over the Promised Land. Paul speaks little of his failed ambition to preach in Bithynia. What we do know is that both Moses and Paul had a choice to make. They could look back bitterly, questioning where it all went wrong, angrily regretting that they ever had dreams at all, and this decision producing tears of disappointment. Or, they can hold their heads up in their disappointment and acknowledge that God has blessed their labor, that in their struggle, God's purposes were advanced and that by God's power, they did step closer to eternal things.

Perhaps there is no greater struggle than recognizing again and again that God's view of success and failure is different from our own. And, it is God's view, which really matters. Moses and Paul fixed their gaze upon a destination. Yet, what really matters to God is whether at the end of the pilgrimage those God calls have learned patience and humility and have entered into an utter dependence upon God. Ultimately, the destination is quite a secondary thing. It is the quality of the pilgrimage that matters. We don't have access to the private thoughts of Moses and Paul as they experienced disappointment. But they were great men of God and great people live their lives for God. I suspect that, at the end of their life, Moses and Paul lifted their gaze beyond failed aspirations and saw God's smile at a life well lived.

Lord, broaden my understanding and make it clearer, so that I may see all of life as you see it and trust my life to your gracious care. Amen.

Is Belief in A Personal God Possible?

"Pray like this: Our Father who is in heaven."
Matthew 6:9 (Common English Bible)

For many, the most challenging part of faith is belief in a personal God. Membership in a local church usually requires "a profession of faith." Often, this is little more than mental consent that there is a God. That same consent to God's existence usually assumes that the individual intends to place themselves under God's authority. Yet, what is often present in that "profession" is a sincere desire to know God personally, to experience a relationship with God in such a manner that in those hours of deepest need, we may personally address God and feel that we are heard and cared for. Harry Emerson Fosdick is helpful here, "No one achieves a vital, personal, Christian experience without a profound sense of need."[12] But the question presses, is belief in a personal God possible?

One difficulty for experiencing a personal God today is the tendency of impersonal thinking and living. Anything sensory is found to be inferior to reason and intelligence. During my ministry in Texas a number of years ago, one individual criticized my preaching as too personal, too emotional. He was a medical doctor and sought sermons that would stretch his thinking, not move his heart. He was suspicious of preaching that stirred the emotions. To think of God in personal terms, he argued, was unsophisticated. I suspect that the Sunday morning pews are filled with people who are in agreement.

But look at what Jesus does here for his disciples: Jesus takes the qualities of human parenting as a clue to understanding God; asks that we address God as father. God is not an impersonal force that moves through the universe. God is a living being that knows us, loves us and has a divine desire for our lives. Jesus draws from what is the best in our hearts to show us its higher ideal in God. Certainly, it is true that God has given us minds and expects that we should be growing in knowledge. But we cannot pursue God and fully know God without the heart. One of the basic convictions of our Christian faith is that the universe is directed by a *loving* purpose.

Moments confront each of us that demand more than a mere belief in the existence of God. They are moments of such great personal need that more study – more knowledge about God – fails to satisfy. A calm strength in the midst of life's storms is possible only as God is known personally. The Christian lives not by a higher knowledge of God. The Christian lives by faith, by prayer, by love and communion with God. When the soul cries out for a personal God, Jesus shows us the way. It is so simple we doubt its power. Get down on your knees, patiently silence all the voices in your mind, and then say, "Our Father, who is in Heaven."

Father, increase my faith in you, and bring my trust to the place you desire that I may be strengthened in your promises and experience the vitality of life you intend. Amen.

---

[12]Harry Emerson Fosdick, **Riverside Sermons** (New York: Harper & Brothers, 1958), 168.

Andrew: The First Disciple

"One of the two disciples who heard what John said and followed Jesus was Andrew, the brother of Simon Peter. He first found his own brother Simon and said to him, 'We have found the Messiah.' He led him to Jesus."
John 1:40-42a (Common English Bible)

John the Baptist was in the wilderness once again preaching that the Kingdom of God was drawing near. But this day would be different. On this day John sighted in the distance, Jesus. And when John's eyes fell upon Jesus there was a spontaneous utterance of his thoughts, "Look! The Lamb of God!" This was all that Andrew, one of John's followers, needed to hear. Instantly, Andrew realized that the object of his longing had now appeared. Andrew and another, unnamed person who was with him, left John and began to follow Jesus. Andrew became the first disciple of Jesus Christ.

Andrew was the first disciple to follow Christ, but little is known about him. John's Gospel tells us that Peter was his brother; the same Peter who would step-out of a boat upon stormy water to approach Jesus, the Peter that Jesus declared would be the rock upon which the church would be built, the Peter who would deny Jesus three times on the night of Jesus' arrest. Yes, that Peter. The gospels provide considerable detail about Andrew's brother, Peter. But of Andrew, we know little. Perhaps, for many ordinary followers of Jesus, Andrew's story is a story of grace. Andrew was not a superstar disciple, not in the sense that he plays a major role in the story of Jesus. But it was Andrew who brought his brother, Peter, to Jesus. Without Andrew, there would be no story of Peter.

John's Gospel only mentions Andrew two other times. On the occasion of Jesus teaching five thousand men, plus women and children, Jesus asks his disciples to provide a meal for the people. The suggestion of feeding so many exhausts the disciples; all the disciples except Andrew, that is. Andrew goes looking for what is available. Andrew simply trusts that anything is possible when Jesus is nearby. In this story, Andrew brings a child to Jesus with the child's meager five loaves of bread and two fish. Then, the final story about Andrew occurs during the last week of Jesus' life. Some Greeks are in town for Passover and are curious about Jesus. The Greeks made inquiry of Philip who introduced them to Andrew, who brought them to Jesus. What little we know of Andrew is enough. Andrew was always bringing people to Jesus.

What is remarkable about the story of Andrew is that there is no evidence that he was ever jealous of the other disciples. Andrew is only mentioned three times in the Gospel of John and in each instance, Andrew brings someone to Jesus and then steps back into the shadows. Andrew never sought, nor received, top billing in the unfolding story of Jesus Christ. It was enough to be used by God to introduce others to Jesus. And then Andrew demonstrated grace in being left behind as the drama of Jesus moved forward. Andrew understood that it wasn't about him. In the end, that just may be the quality that made Andrew one of the greatest disciples.

Compassionate and merciful God, remind me that life is so much greater than my own small desires to be recognized. Help me to be like Andrew, to participate in your great work, in a small or grand manner, without thought of my own reward. Amen.

Sharing Our Faith Story

"Let the redeemed of the Lord say so."
Psalm 107:2 (New Revised Standard Version)

Our daily conversations do more than provide a running narrative of our lives; such conversations shape our experiences, practices and life with one another. As we speak, our thoughts and understandings are more deeply formed and clarified. Through speech, we do so much more than transmit information to another. We process that information in a manner that deepens our convictions. When that conversation turns to matters of faith, my friend Thomas Long, brilliantly observes, "When we talk about our faith, we are not merely expressing our beliefs; we are coming more fully and clearly to believe. In short, we are always talking ourselves into being Christian."[13]

It is uncertain that this is the conviction behind these words from Psalms. What is certain is that God's people are directed to speak of their faith; are commanded to share their faith story with others. It is the duty of every person of faith. The man or woman who has been "redeemed" by the Lord must become a busy person. They are to be messengers of God's love and transformative power. It is this kind of witness that captures the interest of ordinary people and wins their verdict. Clergy are expected to speak of holy things. But when ordinary people speak of God the testimony takes hold with arresting strength and considerable surprise.

But, argues Tom Long, such conversation serves a sacred interest. Speaking with another person about our faith confirms experience; it sustains it and enriches it. Any experience which is denied expression speedily fades away, such as a second language that is never used. The loss may be imperceptible at first but, over time, more and more is lost until little remains. Yet, when voice is given to matters of faith, faith quickens and is given strength. A powerful dynamic is released: as we take hold of our faith, our faith takes hold of us. Doubts melt away like mist when we go public with our testimony of what God has done for us.

The Bible is filled with miracle stories. They are the stories that shape the contours of our faith and reveal God to us; stories that bear witness to God's power. But they are not the stories that are the most vital for living a transformed and transfigured life. The miracle that is most vital, that is most urgent today, is not the miracle that is read about but the one that walks about in every believer who gives confession of their belief. The Lord says, "Let the redeemed of the Lord say so." That is the Lord's command. The world is waiting for our obedience.

Lord, open my heart to a love for all your people. Teach me to pray for them and fill my mouth with the words that speak of your loving kindness to all. Amen.

---

[13] Thomas G. Long, *Testimony: Talking Ourselves into Being Christian* (San Francisco, CA: Jossey-Bass, 2004), 7.

When Christ Knocks

"Look! I'm standing at the door and knocking. If any hear my voice and open the door, I will come in to be with them, and will have dinner with them, and they will have dinner with me."
Revelation 3:20 (Common English Bible)

There comes the moment for each of us when we can no longer deny our inner darkness and weakness, our deficiency against the common struggles of daily life and we become weary. Exhausted, we surrender our grasping to be in control, to be strong and without need for anyone, and we seek something else – a union with some strength and purpose beyond ourselves. This verse from Revelation comes to us at such moments. Here we are told that Jesus stands at the door and is ready to come in, if we allow it, and to take possession of our lives, to recreate our inner life and fill it with light and strength. As we stop grasping and are, rather, grasped by Jesus, we are gradually lifted by him, in spite of ourselves, and, from degree to degree, changed into the likeness of Christ.

For this to proceed in our own life we must first recognize the knock of Jesus. How is that done? It may not be immediately recognizable. It may only be a vague sense of dissatisfaction with the movement of your life; a growing discomfort with the hopes, desires and ambitions that have fueled your daily decisions. Perhaps the knock is found in protest, deep in your heart, about what others are saying to you about this, or that, or another person, and you sense that all of it is wrong. Something stirs within you for another conversation, one that is nobler, more loving, and lovelier. It may even be the Christ-like manner you witness in another and find that you desire to share in that behavior. The knock may simply be an impulse, a nudge, a longing of the heart.

But to recognize the knock is insufficient. It is inconceivable that anyone would hear a knock on the front door of their home and simply ignore it. To ignore an unsettled heart is just as inconceivable. A knock demands to be answered, the door opened. What stands on the other side may be refused but it must be acknowledged. For a disciple, the door is opened, and Christ is admitted at once. There should be no postponement. A postponement weakens the spirit and may result in missing Christ altogether, Christ possibly never returning again. To welcome Christ is to learn of him, to listen deeply to what he teaches and then to obey all that we understand of him. It is to acknowledge that life without Christ was failing us and to utterly reject any notion of negotiating with what Christ demands.

What remains is a promise. The person, who hears the knock, opens the door and admits Christ into the inner place of their life discovers a deep and abiding communion with him, "and (I) will have dinner with them, and they will have dinner with me." This is a relationship with Christ that moves way beyond simple obedience. It is the richest and most intimate of relationships; a relationship where one heart deeply shapes the heart of another and two are like one. Christ becomes more than a savior. Christ becomes one who makes us a better person and shares the journey of life as a contemporary, providing life with a peace and joy and adequacy that is simply unavailable without him.

Tune my ears to the sound of your knock, O God, and make me swift to respond that I may know the peace and joy you promise. Amen.

Experiencing A Real and Vivid Faith

"Taste and see how good the Lord is! The one who takes refuge in him is truly happy!"
Psalm 34:8 (Common English Bible)

There are large numbers of people who have never experienced faith as a matter of the heart – a stirring of the emotions. They have a good mind, a strong character, and possess a genuine love for God. Yet, their faith is lived as a mental consent to the teachings of the Bible, the Church, and others who are respected and admired. What they lack – and may long for – is a genuine, personal encounter with the living God, a personal engagement with the holy.

Some time ago, I was sharing breakfast with a friend and we were discussing the story from Genesis where Jacob wrestled with God throughout the night. *"When the man (God) saw that he couldn't defeat Jacob, he grabbed Jacob's thigh and tore a muscle in Jacob's thigh as he wrestled with him.* (Genesis 32:25)" My friend uttered impulsively – and sincerely – "I would be happy to walk with a limp to have had that kind of experience with God!"

A rare opportunity presented itself years ago for my wife and me to be present in the studio during the taping of Good Morning America. Emeril Lagasse was a guest of the show that particular morning. Sam Champion asked me to accompany him as Emeril demonstrated the preparation of a holiday dessert. At the conclusion of the demonstration, Emeril invited Champion to "taste" what they had created together. Sam Champion did and the look on Champion's face pleased Emeril. What happened next was unexpected. Champion grabbed another fork, cut another "taste" from the dessert and held it to my mouth: "Doug, you have got to taste this!" I had two choices – the studio camera now on me as a national audience watched. I could demand that Champion prove to me it was as good as he seemed to think before I opened my mouth, or I could simply "taste" and see for myself. Naturally, I did the latter. My conclusion concurred with Champion's. It was perhaps the best dessert I had ever tasted.

Robert J. McCracken has observed that the experience of faith occurs in a similar manner, "It begins as an experiment and ends as an experience."[14] McCracken says that too often faith is not lived authentically – an earnest effort each day to have our lives shaped by the teachings of Jesus. What remains is a faith that receives intellectual consent and lives in argument of what the Bible really teaches. A substitution is required. Substitute the practice of faith for argument and, in time, both a religious experience and conviction will be yours. Christ has pledged that it will be so.

Heavenly Father, for too long have I allowed myself to be hampered, hobbled and crippled by weakness of faith. Stir me once again by your great power that I may rise out of a dull faith and experience the real and vivid faith promised in scripture. Amen.

---

[14]Robert J. McCracken, "How Does One Acquire Religious Experience?" *Questions People Ask: Sermons Preached in Riverside Church, New York City* (New York: Harper & Brothers, 1951), 17.

Disagreements in the Church

"They capture every thought to make it obedient to Christ."
2 Corinthians 10:5 (Common English Bible)

If you read – and listen – carefully to Paul's letters to the church in Corinth, you might be surprised. Paul had a contentious relationship with that church. Frankly, what you find in 1st and 2nd Corinthians is far richer and more dynamic than the story lines of today's soap operas. That congregation simply didn't like Paul, and his feelings for them seemed mutual. Hate would be an overstatement but certainly there was present a strong dislike for one another.

Actually, it may not be fair to charge Paul with a strong dislike for the Corinthian church. They drove him crazy like no other church. He was frustrated to the point of over-heating on many occasions. His angst with this church is palpable in his two letters. They were incorrigible, no question. But he never walked away from them, he never dismissed them. I think the reason he loved them in spite of their behavior was that he saw himself in them. There is ample evidence in Paul's other writings that he was also stubborn, incorrigible and intractable. But Paul loved Jesus. And he wanted this church to love Jesus as well.

Reading Paul's letters to this church demonstrates two powerful lessons to the church of today: the first is that occasionally good Christians might disagree. The second is that when we do disagree, we are to handle those disagreements differently from the way everyone else does. What non-Christians tend to do is draw lines in the sand, spin the facts to slant in our direction and take down the opposition as fast as we can. In this passage of scripture, Paul urges a different path: *"capture every thought to make it obedient to Christ."* Simply, Paul is asking that we include Jesus in the conversation, seeking wisdom from him.

What this means, of course, is that we must have some humility in our disagreements. This is hard. It is human nature to be absolutely convinced that we are right, and others are wrong. So Paul reminds us that in our baptism we submit to the Lordship of Jesus in all things – even when we think we are right. The question then becomes what is most important, demonstrating that we are right at any cost or humbling ourselves before Christ and acknowledging that there may be more truth than we once realized.

Forgive me, Heavenly Father, when I insist upon my own way before listening carefully to another. Help me to surrender all disagreements to the Lordship of Jesus Christ. Amen.

Remember

"Don't forget the covenant that the Lord your God made with you..."
Deuteronomy 4:23b (Common English Bible)

The word, "remember" has taken on fresh poignancy for the citizens of the United States. Recently, our nation observed the fifteenth anniversary of the terrorist attack in New York, Pennsylvania, and Washington, D.C. Commonly referenced as 9/11, the entering High School freshman class this year is the first class to begin High School who was born after these attacks. It is all history to them. Why is it important to teach these young students what happened that September day before they were born? Foremost, it is important because it is a critical part of our shared story as U.S. citizens. That single incident has dramatically reshaped the landscape of how we live today. Secondly, the story keeps all of us wide-eyed of what occurs each day around the world and how our lives may be impacted.

Here in Deuteronomy, Moses asks the people of God to "remember." Remember their slavery in Egypt. Remember God's leadership, and care for them, as they traveled from Egypt, through the wilderness, to a new land that will be their home. Remember, because all that history has shaped them as a people; has shaped them as a nation. If they are to have any understanding of their identity, they must remember who they were and God's mighty acts among them. Just as important, their future is filled with uncertainties – as is any future – and the very act of "recalling" God's presence and care in the past strengthens them for whatever they would face moving forward. "Don't forget the covenant that the Lord your God made with you."

This is an important reason for our regular worship and personal reading of the Bible. Like the nation of Israel, we also must remember. In those times when our life has reached the depths of disappointment and struggle, it is easy to remember; to remember and call out to God for help. But when life is sailing from one beautiful shore to the next, difficulty is at a minimum and resources to meet any emotional or physical need are abundant, remembering God is difficult. Little by little, a notion expands upon our consciousness that God can be dispensed with. The tragic result is to face the future alone, with only our strength. Eventually, that strength will be insufficient.

Perhaps a greater concern is that when a nation loses its faith, a sense that each of us belong to something bigger than the present moment, that nation ceases to be a nation at all. What is left is a lot of people milling around with no larger story arc than their own small lives, going nowhere. It is important to remember origins, to remember where we came from and how we got here. This memory dispenses the lie that we made something out of our lives from nothing. Memory becomes the source and impulse to new life; a life full of hope and promise for the future. And the nation that recovers a sense of responsibility, under God, discovers a divine purpose that strengthens the bonds that binds one to another and thrusts it forward into the future with confident expectation.

Heavenly Father, help me remember that I am a member of a great family. Grant me a fresh awareness of your claim upon me and the future you call me toward. In Christ's name, I pray. Amen.

For This Moment

*"In fact, if you don't speak up at this very important time,
relief and rescue will appear for the Jews from another place."*
Esther 4:14 (Common English Bible)

Esther is a Jew who, by some unusual circumstances, becomes the queen of Persia. Additionally, by other unusual circumstances, Esther is able to discover a plot to assassinate the king. By alerting the king, she earns his deep gratitude. A cursory reading of this short story in the Old Testament reveals one unusual turn after another.

Then, near the middle of this unusual story, Esther stumbles upon plans to exterminate all the Jews throughout the empire. Not only does she uncover this plot to destroy her people, Esther realizes that she is the only person who can potentially stop it. There is a difficulty, however. According to the laws of the empire in that day, the one thing Esther must do to save her people could result in the loss of everything Esther treasures. Short stories don't get better than this.

Naturally, Esther struggles with what she should do; play it safe and watch her people die or take a risk and potentially lose her own life. At this moment, Esther's uncle shows up and speaks these words to her, *"In fact, if you don't speak up at this very important time, relief and rescue will appear for the Jews from another place."* Simply, Esther's uncle is telling her that it may well be that God has arranged for Esther to be queen for just this moment. More importantly, God will act to save his people with or without Esther.

At the end of this nail-biting story, the reader is left with the distinct possibility that unusual turns in life are not really random. God is very much a part of our lives. When we discover unusual circumstances or opportunities presented to us, we may well ask, "What would you have me do for this moment, O Lord?" Obedience or disobedience? It is the grand question of the ages.

Open my eyes this day, O God, to your wondrous presence and activity in my life. Show me what you would have me do and grant me the courage for obedience. Amen.

Disillusionment with God

*"The burning sand will become a pool,
and the thirsty ground, fountains of water."*
Isaiah 35:7 (Common English Bible)

There is, perhaps, no greater disappointment in life than to experience disappointment with God. Missed opportunities, unrealized dreams and friends who fail us are no small matter. They can be debilitating at times. Yet, most people also recognize that such disappointments are the stuff of life. With a strong network of family and friends, many find that they are able to push through such disappointments. But what are we to do with our disappointment with God? This is the most shattering of disappointments. "No longer is there a wide, comfortable margin between peace and the edge of doom," writes that great Scottish preacher, James S. Steward.[15] Disillusionment with God is startling, surprising and overwhelming. In a deep spiritual sense, such disillusionment is taking-up residence in the desert.

Isaiah has a word for those desert moments – or days. In dramatic fashion, Isaiah speaks of a grand reversal, "The burning sand will become a pool, and the thirsty ground, fountains of water." With incredible verve, he takes the most frightening and cynical judgment of the world that says that this life is nothing more than "burning sand" and reverses it. God is not absent, nor will God remain silent. The word from the Lord is that the desert places of life will become an oasis; living water that quenches our fears and dispels the darkness.

What does this mean? In effect, Isaiah acknowledges his common experience with ours that life is full of disappointments, broken dreams and dashed hopes. More, Isaiah is no stranger to fears that come like a bolt of lightning, unnerving our sense of comfort and security. But he also wants to remind us of history; Israel's history of a God that is never far off, a God that appears in the midst of struggle and uncertainty with the hand of a shepherd, confidently leading us forward into God's future for us. In every situation, even when the darkness of the hour seems to have the upper hand, grace reigns.

Understand, of course, that the very struggle with disillusionment dispels any notion that faith is always experienced without struggle. Any spiritual journey occasionally moves through desert places, where the ground is hot and parched. But, Isaiah asks that we steadily move forward, particularly when our steps are labored and weak, for a wonderful discovery lies ahead of us, the same discovery that Isaiah made. Present circumstances that seem as burning sand will, by God's promises, become a pool of cool water. Additionally, you will find yourself in the company of those who have discovered that they would rather travel the most difficult road with God than any other road without him.

Forgive my disillusionment, O Lord, and restore my heart to the certain knowledge that, in the midst of difficulty, you are present. Amen.

---

[15]James S. Stewart, "Beyond Disillusionment to Faith," *The Wind of the Spirit* (Nashville and New York: Abingdon Press, 1968), 70.

Recovering the Adventure of Faith

*"Instead, dress yourself with the Lord Jesus Christ,
and don't plan to indulge your selfish desires."*
Romans 13:14 (Common English Bible)

For some, the experience of the Christian faith lacks the heroic and adventurous texture of the lives of great biblical personalities. Safe, comfortable boredom is more often presented today in the life of those who follow Christ. Absent are uncalculated risks, the thrill of battling difficulties and the appetite for conflict and victory. The faith has become soft, the individual life one of self-indulgent behavior. The demands of scripture go unnoticed, perhaps on purpose, and everything is made too easy. The casualty is a faith without power or interest.

In more honest moments, such people will often confess to a desire for something more, something deeper. A world of risk and adventure is preferred over the predictable routines that our lives fall into. The zest of struggle and conquest teases our minds and the ever-present possibility of calamity and pain doesn't diminish the lure. Rather, these are the factors which make possible human happiness; joy the product of discipline and effort.

Such a faith remains within the reach of anyone who desires it. It arrives along the route of spiritual discipline. Unlike military discipline, a discipline that is imposed from without, spiritual discipline emerges from within. It is self-imposed. It builds spiritual muscle that is revealed in unquestionable character and contagious personalities. Discipline may seem, for a time, to be a thing of pain and not joy, but those who are trained by it are quick to demonstrate a life that is stronger, healthier and marked by joyful anticipation. Faith, properly experienced, becomes life's grandest adventure.

Those who endeavor to claim such an experience of faith are addressed in these few words from Romans, "dress yourself with the Lord Jesus Christ." The daily discipline of arising from bed and dressing our bodies with clothes appropriate for the day is purposely chosen. Dress the spiritual body each morning, as the physical body is dressed. Strive to eliminate unchristian attitudes and thoughts and consider how to be more loving of others. Remain alert to the needs of others and less preoccupied with your own. And do not neglect the regular reading and reflection upon God's Word in the Bible. Think of how to please Christ throughout the day and such strength of faith as never known before will be given to you.

Thank you, Heavenly Father, for each new day. Empty my heart of fear and fill it full of you, in whose presence there can be no apprehension. Restore the adventure of faith that is discovered in practicing your presence throughout the day. Amen.

More from Jesus

"But Jesus said to them, 'Prophets are honored everywhere except in their own hometowns and in their own households.' He was unable to do many miracles there because of their disbelief."
Matthew 13:57-58 (Common English Bible)

The wonderful preacher, Barbara Brown Taylor once observed that Jesus' power was not diminished in Nazareth due to unbelief. He was still the same person. The reason Jesus wasn't able to do much there was because they would not let him. "If you ever pressed a lit match to a pile of wet sticks," writes Taylor, "then you know what it was like. It does not matter how strong your flame is: what you need is something that will catch fire."[16]

We have become accustomed to thinking about the power of faith. What we may not realize is that unbelief has power as well. This is the power demonstrated here in this story from Matthew. Jesus grew up in Nazareth. The people recognized him as the child who became a carpenter. The people's familiarity with Jesus resulted in disbelief – disbelief that anything special could be done by him. They knew Jesus so well that it was inconceivable that God could be at work in the commonplace.

Unfortunately, many of us are from Jesus' hometown of Nazareth. We have grown-up with Jesus. Attendance in Sunday School since an early age, a family Bible prominent in our homes and regular worship has made Jesus quite familiar to us. And for some, this familiarity has diminished our expectation of what Jesus can do. With diminished expectations comes diminished experience of the supernatural.

Perhaps that is why I always look for opportunities to be around those new to the faith. They sense that there is more to Jesus than many realize. Much more. And until each of us come to see that, we will continue to expect little from Jesus. As the biblical scholar, Douglas R.A. Hare has noted, "God's power is unlimited, but its expression is correlated with the response of faith. Those who expect nothing from God will not be disappointed."[17]

Forgive me when I expect little from you, Heavenly Father. Lift my eyes to see the possibilities you see for my life. Amen.

---

[16]Barbara Brown Taylor, ***Bread of Angels*** (Boston, MA: Cowley Publications, 1997), 105.

[17]Douglas R.A. Hare, ***Mark*** (Louisville, KY: Westminster John Knox Press, 1996), 70.

The Ultimate Source of Greatness

*"All who lift themselves up will be brought low,
and those who make themselves low will be lifted up."*
Luke 18:14b (Common English Bible)

Every culture holds up its ideal of beauty, success and power. Similarly, every culture is judged by what it values. The type of person on whom our culture bestows recognition and honor is not easily missed. Magazine covers celebrate beauty, Jennifer Aniston named most beautiful woman by People Magazine, those who epitomize success on the cover of Success Magazine and those who command power in leadership on the magazine cover of Fast Company. Bestsellers are indicative of the trends and tastes of the culture and advertisements of luxury items promise success, or the illusion of success, to those who can afford the purchase.

Jesus had a great deal to say about success and seeking status, "All who lift themselves up will be brought low, and those who make themselves low will be lifted up." In these few words, Jesus questions the nature of our ambition; the character of the success we seek. Simply, Jesus asks, "What are any of us really after?" More deeply, Jesus questions where in our life plan does God come in? Do we imagine ourselves self-sufficient? Or do we recognize that God is the beginning and the end of everything, including our lives?

It is important to listen carefully to Jesus' teachings, however, and notice that it isn't human littleness that Jesus stresses but efforts of self-aggrandizement and grandeur. Often, we strive to go it alone, living our lives under our own power, making our own way, and if successful, grandly announce that we are self-made. All things, including other people, are subordinated to our own purposes and designs. There exists only one purpose in all our efforts – to get out of life all we can get. What we fail to grasp is that we are not here to live as we please, and to obtain all that we desire, but to live in a manner that pleases God and adds value to the lives of others.

Ours is an unspiritual culture. Though there may remain great numbers of people on church membership rolls, many of these same people speak and act in almost complete independence of God, as though God didn't exist, or doesn't really matter. They are led by their own desires to a shallow and superficial life. For Jesus this was not so. He was conscious of God each moment of the day, every decision made in devoted obedience to his heavenly Father. For Jesus, there could be no greatness apart from God, recognizing that God is the ultimate source of greatness. And it is that insight that Jesus most urgently wishes to convey here in these few words.

Rescue me from a shallow and superficial life, a life that is filled with those things that perish. Show me again the beauty of a life lived for you and your kingdom's work throughout the world. Amen.

Where to Begin

"Rather, you will receive power when the Holy Spirit has come upon you, and you will be my witnesses in Jerusalem, in all Judea and Samaria, and to the end of the earth."
Acts 1:8 (Common English Bible)

When the king in *Alice in Wonderland* was asked where to begin, he said gravely, "Begin at the beginning… and go on till you come to the end: then stop." Begin at the beginning. Naturally, that guidance seems reasonable. That is, until you have to actually open your mouth, and speak. With thoughts racing from one place to another, it quickly becomes apparent that there are many fine places to begin. Jesus tells his disciples, here in Acts, "you will be my witnesses." Where do the disciples begin? Where are we to begin? Sharing our faith in Jesus seems reasonable until we actually confront that moment – that moment when we are asked, "Who is Jesus?"

That moment came to me one Easter morning. I was enjoying breakfast in a Doylestown, PA diner, looking over the message I would preach in just a few hours. Mary, the waitress assigned to the table where I was seated, approached with coffee and said, "I guess this is your big day, pastor!" "I guess so," I remarked. Then Mary asked, "What is Easter all about anyway?" Initially, I dismissed her question, not thinking she was serious. But I was mistaken; Mary was very serious. It was then I took the time to really notice her, to look into her eyes and really see her. I will not forget those eyes - eyes that betrayed her silence; silence of considerable pain. "Where do I begin?" I thought. I began with her pain. "Easter means that you can stop beating yourself up. Whatever guilt you may have now, whatever mistakes you have made in life, Easter means that you are to stop immediately from beating yourself up. God has removed it all."

"But there is more," I said to Mary. "Easter is an invitation to pay attention to Jesus." I shared with Mary that as she paid attention to Jesus, by reading of him in the Bible, she will discover that she will want to be more than she is now. "Pay attention long enough to Jesus and you will experience a compulsion to be something more; you will begin to live differently." Mary needed to hear that Jesus doesn't leave a life unchanged. Any significant time spent with Jesus always results in a desire to be made new. "Your whole world will appear different. You will want to be different."

"Finally, Mary, begin to follow Jesus as you learn about him." I shared with her that what that means is to "do what he asks in his teaching." Imagine Jesus as a mentor in life and do everything that is asked of you. Something inexplicable happens when someone commits to doing all that Jesus' asks: they receive an uncommon power to do so. People who obey all that they understand of Jesus' teachings receive a power from outside of themselves; a power that actually makes them something so much more than what they were. Mary began to cry and asked how to begin. That is when I knew I had come to the end. And there, in a diner in Doylestown, PA, Mary gave her life to Jesus.

Holy Spirit, pull me back from a preoccupation with myself to a world of lonely, desperate people; people who still wait to hear the Good News of Jesus Christ. Fill me with the compassion of Christ and direct my witness of Christ's promises to them. Amen.

Loving God with Our Minds

"...and you must love the Lord your God with all your heart, with all your being, with all your mind, and with all your strength."
Mark 12:30 (Common English Bible)

These words are a portion of Jesus' great commandment. Here Jesus emphatically declares that there is a place in the exercise of faith for using our minds. God wants our heads as well as our hearts. Beautiful, compelling worship stirs the heart and encourages the spirit – the organ, the piano and the singing of the great hymns of the church. But what of our minds? God's desire is that our minds be kindled as well. Placing our minds into the service of God is every bit as necessary as private prayer and public worship. What Jesus makes clear is that when God claims a person, God claims the whole person.

When women and men put their minds to work in the service of God things begin to happen. One powerful dynamic is the movement, from one degree to another, of a greater understanding of God and God's purposes within the church and the world. There is a powerful pull within many people of faith to keep belief fixed and static. The pursuit of a deeper understanding of scripture and grasp of truth is threatening. Old, cherished understandings of the faith are familiar and comfortable. Yet, the fear of new discoveries of God's truth may be, in fact, disobedience to God; the choosing to worship a God that fits nicely into our preferred set of beliefs rather than the God who is revealed in the pursuit of truth.

The application of our minds to the exercise of faith also results in an enlarged capacity to discern God's will for our lives. Ephesians 2:10 teaches that God created each person "to do good things." The quest for each person of faith must be the rich discovery of God's specific purpose for their life; the understanding of what "good things" are expected from a person committed to the Lordship of Jesus Christ. The deep study of scripture and reflection on where God may be in the world gives clarity about the things that matter most. Asking no questions and the refusal to pursue truth wherever truth may lead is a dangerous course. Satan's temptation of Jesus failed, in part, because Jesus applied his mind to knowing God.

Recently, a man sat in my office and declared that the Presbyterian faith of today was, in fact, a large departure from the faith he cherished ten years ago. He was experiencing a mixture of disorientation and anger. The denomination has taken theological positions he simply could not agree with. I found his comment, "The church has left me" to be unsettling. Perhaps the church has left him. If this otherwise intelligent man has chosen to keep his belief fixed and without the exercise of healthy inquiry, the church has moved on. The church does get it wrong from time to time, that is certain. But I celebrate participation in a community of faith that courageously seeks new understandings of a God that continues to surprise us.

Father, thank you for hearts to love you and minds to search the riches of your wisdom. Grant me understanding of your will and the humility to remain open to fresh knowledge of your wondrous work in the world. Amen.

The Weight of Guilt

"Come to me, all you who are struggling hard and carrying heavy loads, and I will give you rest. Put on my yoke, and learn from me. I'm gentle and humble. And you will find rest for yourselves."
Matthew 11: 28, 29 (Common English Bible)

During my recent trip to the Holy Land I saw a donkey carrying a heavy load, with heaving sides and hanging its head, it's strength almost spent. It appeared as though this animal was ready to sink. Certainly, Jesus saw something similar. A master teacher, Jesus would take what was familiar to the people of his day, point to it, and then make use of it as an object lesson for opening-up the great truths of God's presence and work. A donkey, struggling hard under the weight of a heavy load, may be the object lesson here in these few sentences of Matthew's Gospel.

There are moments in our life when we know the burden of that donkey. We struggle hard, carry heavy loads and our bodies – and spirit – become weary. Our strength is not equal to the weight. We feel as though we will sink under it all. It is precisely at that moment, the moment we fear that we will collapse, that Jesus promises "rest." There is an intense force and allure to this gracious promise. When our own strength has been spent, Jesus shows-up. And our gigantic weight, whatever it may be, is made manageable once again.

I am convinced that of the scattered army of things that weigh heavily upon the human heart, none is greater than guilt. There is no exhaustion like the exhaustion created by guilt. It marshals our best efforts to defeat it only to exact a terrible drain upon our energies, dragging many into hopelessness and despair. What I am now certain of is that there is only one hope for those sinking beneath the crushing weight of guilt. It is found in the infinite power of divine forgiveness, the forgiveness of Jesus Christ.

Jesus' invitation is, "Come to me." So rest is to be gained by finding Christ. Pay attention to Christ long enough and what will be discovered is that Christ himself found rest in his heavenly Father. What's more, that rest he found was sought each day. Jesus never was content to live on stale grace from his Father. It was sought fresh each day. So that is our example. Christ wants his gift of "rest" to be a daily find; something we seek from him each day. And that is how it is to be retained, seeking it day after day. Christ's desire is that life will be a prolonged spiritual quest, seeking Christ and knowing Christ more fully each day. It will be then that the weight of guilt is removed and rest is found.

Wondrous and merciful God, thank you that amidst the confusion and conflict of daily life, you speak a clear and simple truth: in Jesus Christ, we are separated from our sins and are made free from our guilt. Amen.

An Indecisive Faith

*"Elijah approached all the people and said,
'How long will you hobble back and forth between two opinions? If the Lord is
God, follow God. If Baal is God, follow Baal.' The people gave no answer."*
I Kings 18:21 (Common English Bible)

There are multitudes of people today who live with an indecisive faith. In their heart of hearts, they want to believe that they are a people of belief. For Christians, they may belong to a local church, worship regularly and participate in the financial support of the church. They possess a Bible – perhaps several – and may read it regularly. But when opportunities are presented for them to take a stand for what they know is right, what they know is a Christian position, they become hesitant. They are afraid to publicly confess that they follow the Lord, Jesus Christ, and intend to honor Christ in each of their decisions. No one who knows them can be certain just where they stand.

This spirit of hesitation is far removed from the heroism of first century Christianity. In the Book of Acts, we encounter another story, the story of Christians who are arrested and beaten for their faith. When they are at last released from prison they are given the express command never to speak of Christ again. This warning does not stop them. Their faith is not dubious, hesitant, or vacillating. Just the opposite is true. We read that daily in the temple and in every house, they never ceased to teach and preach Jesus Christ. They are followers of Jesus Christ who make their life and influence count in the struggle of right and wrong.

Why should we hesitate to affirm our faith as these first century Christians? If we believe in God and are sincere in our desire to follow Jesus as Lord of our lives, why not say so? The conviction of the Christian faith is that the establishment of God's Kingdom would bring a better world. Only a few hundred Christians with a faith as resolute and unwavering as these first century Christians would have the capacity to stir any local community to its foundations. But what happens often today is that people "hobble back and forth between two opinions." Either they are uncertain or are ashamed of their convictions as followers of Jesus.

Elijah challenged the people of Israel to take a stand, one way or another. We are similarly challenged by his words. Cease to "hobble back and forth" and, rather, take a stand for something, either for the God we know in the person of Jesus or for something else. Someone once said, "Show me a man's checkbook and I will tell you the name of his god." I am confident that Elijah wouldn't need their checkbook. How we speak, the manner in which we treat one another and the decisions we make – particularly moral and business decisions – demonstrate who or what is Lord of our lives. What a pity that anyone who has ever named Jesus as Lord would be found by others as a person of indecisive faith.

Father of Abraham and Moses, of Paul and Peter, you continue to call people to yourself and to nurture within them a faith that can move mountains. Forgive me when I am hesitant to share with others my hope in Jesus Christ and fill my heart with expectant joy that is unquenchable. Amen.

Overwhelmed?

"God's word continued to grow and increase."
Acts 12:24 (Common English Bible)

On the streets, in our neighborhoods and our places of work the prevailing mood of the day is, "overwhelmed". The world today seems to be more complex, more massive, and more unmanageable than our individual and corporate memory can recall. The magnitude of the problems we face as a nation – particularly threats to our national security – leave us bewildered and frightened. It seems that we are up against a new level of massiveness and everything now appears to be beyond the power of ordinary people and governments to solve or control. Confronted with the overwhelming complexities of life today, the question presses against our hearts and spirits, is there hope?

This one sentence from the Book of Acts does not suggest a solution to the enormity of the difficulties we face. It does suggest the mood created by them. As the church, as followers of Jesus Christ, we have a responsibility to our families, our colleagues and the communities in which we live to shift the focus from the staggering weight of our nation's ills to a mood of optimism. It is not "wishful thinking" that is suggested by this one verse in Acts. Rather, it is the evidence that, in a world of mounting difficulties, God remains active and in control. What is most urgently needed today is for the church to be the church, to change the present mood of being overwhelmed to one of conviction that God has come into the world and that God's Word continues to grow and increase.

The world in which these words were written was not unlike our own. The church of Jesus Christ was under a most severe persecution and its continued existence seemed doubtful. King Herod is on a rampage to stamp-out the church by destroying its leaders. Peter and John are placed in prison. James, the brother of John, is killed, and the church is under constant attack and is being scattered everywhere. But, God's word continued to grow and increase. This truth, the unfaltering movement of God's Word, is a tonic for the timid and an encouragement for each one of us who feel overwhelmed.

As the church, as members of the body of Christ, we have a moral and faithful obligation to reevaluate our mood. Since the world tends to magnify the negative, a Christian mood of hope is vital. When some ask, "What is this world coming to?" the church must answer, "Christ has come into the world." It is that response that changes the prevailing mood. It may not be within our power to control the conditions of life, but we do have a choice for our attitude toward them. What is now needed is a new approach. The church's high calling is to strengthen people by our unwavering confidence that, in the midst of unsettling news, God is not absent.

Quiet my anxiety, Heavenly Father, and remind me again of the simple truth that your love for me is already present. In the name of Jesus Christ, I pray. Amen.

The Power of Purpose

"I'm doing important work, so I can't come down."
Nehemiah 6:3 (Common English Bible)

The absence of success isn't the great malady of our time; it is the absence of purpose. Millions of men and women push through each day eking out a living with no large meaning or compelling purpose in life to inspire them. Each day they are going and going but are not moving toward anything. Without direction or motivation these people find their lives flattened, living lives that are meaningless and without a center that strengthens both physically and emotionally. Life is little more than some sort of dreary treadmill; the result being that powers are depleted and personal existence seemingly pointless. These are people who will say that, more than comfort or security, what they crave most of all is meaning in their lives.

Nehemiah found the answer to aimlessness, "I'm doing important work, so I can't come down." Nehemiah put his hand out to a task that God wanted done and no distraction or discouragement would pull him away from that work. Naturally, Nehemiah's first task was to properly discern what it was that God wanted from him. The exercise of discovering God's purpose for us is commonly called, spiritual formation. It need not be a complicated process, but it does require a determination of the heart and a regular time commitment. At the minimum, what is necessary is the regular reading of the Bible and the prayer, "What would you have me hear from these words and what would you have me to do?"

This is a large message of the New Testament; that salvation is, in part, being delivered from aimlessness and finding our lives organized around the creative purposes of God. Attention to God's voice in the Bible gathers the scattered forces of our being and links them to the one divine force at work in the world. Anyone who has spent considerable time with God in this manner discovers that their loyalties are shaped and a grand purpose in life emerges. Day then follows day with a deep sense of meaning running through each of them because these people finally discover that they are moving steadily toward something worth getting to.

When people say that they are going to pieces, often they are speaking the literal truth. Life has a tendency to crumble into pieces when a centering purpose is absent. What is deeply needed is some master passion, some supreme devotion that will hold our scattered selves together. That is the enormous contribution that Christ makes in the world. Christ puts divine meaning into our daily human tasks and saves us from scattered, aimless living. Called to a great cause, a great enterprise worthy of our complete devotion, fractured lives are once again pulled together, physical energies restored, and we discover that we are caught-up in an important work. It is a work that recovers purpose and makes us whole.

Great God, you offer such big purposes to such small people. Grant to me the vision and capacity to live the big life you intend for me. Help me to remember once again that by your power, all things are possible. Amen.

Christmas Confidence

"But right now, we don't see everything under their control yet. However, we do see the one who was made lower in order than the angels for a little while – it's Jesus!"
Portions of Hebrews 2:8, 9 (Common English Bible)

This Christmas season finds us rather bewildered, facing confusion, uncertainty and fear. The world seems dangerously out of control and political leaders have failed to offer a neat formula that can solve our problems or allay our anxiety. We seem a long way from the promise of Isaiah that instruments of war will become farming equipment. But as Christmas draws near, Hebrews reminds us of a man who lived in a world not unlike our own, and yet, carried with him hope and confidence – Jesus Christ. Specifically, Hebrews tells us that we may not yet see everything "under control" but we do see Jesus!

Harry Emerson Fosdick once commented that in pointing to Jesus, Hebrews does not seek to distract us from realistic facts to a beautiful ideal; Hebrews is simply turning our attention from one set of facts to another fact. Jesus is a fact. He lived and his life left an indelible imprint upon the world. Some may question the nature of Jesus, may question the identity of Jesus as anything more than a mortal, but few question that Jesus lived. Yet, women and men of faith accept Jesus as more; accept, as fact, that Jesus is God's decisive interruption in history to bring all things "under control". Jesus is a towering, challenging, revealing fact that casts a whole new outlook on the present groaning of life today.

In this season of Advent – a season of anticipation – those faithful to the Lordship of Jesus see something tremendous occurring in the midst of the daily news: they see the emergence of a disruptive force that will overcome the wild, uncivilized and uncontrolled powers that tear at the world. In the birth of Jesus, God announces that the forces of darkness now have reason to tremble. No, we do not yet see all things "under control" – far from it – but we do see Jesus! And that means that God is on the move.

Our world today is one where fear seems to grow unchecked and uncertainty enlarges upon our consciousness. But God has come in Jesus to change the whole complexion of the world. What is required is that we open ourselves to Jesus in a manner that he can get at us and live in us so that he shapes our thoughts and behavior. One person of faith after another, opening their hearts and minds to receive the transforming power of God, makes all the difference in the world. That is our Christmas confidence.

Open my heart, soul, and mind to a fresh infusion of Christ's love and power that doubt is driven from me and my life today is secured in you. Amen.

When We Are Desperate

"I'm in trouble if I don't preach the gospel."
1 Corinthians 9:16 (Common English Bible)

John Sutherland Bonnell, that wonderful preacher of the Fifth Avenue Presbyterian Church in New York City, from 1935 until his retirement in 1962, once shared with that congregation that there is very present among many pastors a crisis of identity. Simply, many pastors have arrived at the conclusion that they could make a greater contribution by going into politics, medicine or some other vocation than ministry. Pastors today have the uneasy feeling that the ministry of Jesus Christ has been relegated to a secondary place in usefulness to the greater good and service of others.

This was my experience one December night fifteen years ago. I served a congregation in Irving, Texas and a dear member of that church was very ill. My visit with her in the Irving Memorial Hospital that evening left me troubled. I held her hand; I read several Psalms of comfort from the Bible and prayed with her. Before leaving her room, I told her that I loved her. I did love her – deeply so. Her weeks in the hospital and my frequent visits had brought us very close to one another. Now it seemed that she would not return home. She was dying. And there was nothing I could do for her. I had the uneasy feeling that I had little to contribute.

My black, leatherbound Bible was clutched tightly in my hand as I stood in an elevator for the ride down to the lobby. Before the doors closed, a doctor stepped onto the elevator with me. He gave me a pleasant smile as he took a place next to me. He stood there in his white jacket, identity badge attached and a stethoscope around his neck. I remember how intensely I wished I could trade my Bible for his stethoscope – I wanted to be useful to my friend. The doors of the elevator closed.

Then the doctor spoke to me. "Are you a pastor?" I felt inadequate as I answered that I was. "Would you pray for me?" he asked. "I am going now to care for someone who is desperately ill. I have given her the best care my training and experience can give, yet she remains very sick. I have neither the strength nor skills to do more. I need

Jesus now. She needs Jesus now. Would you pray for me, for her?"

Tonight is Christmas Eve. Tonight the church stands on tiptoe anticipating one who comes to us when our strength is depleted and our skills are inadequate. God comes to us in Jesus precisely because our best politics, our best medicine, aren't sufficient for our need. The Apostle Paul understood this. Paul's conception of ministry, says Bonnell, is separate from ours as far as the east is from the west. Paul had a firm grasp of our need. So he preached the gospel.

Pierce my heart today with the amazing power of your love and comfort, O God. In the certain name of your Son, my Lord, Jesus Christ. Amen.

What Are We to Do with Our Fears?

"He said, 'Father, if it's your will, take this cup of suffering away from me. However, not my will but your will must be done.'"
Luke 22:42 (Common English Bible)

Fear is an area of human experience, which involves us all. Fear shows no partiality. The young and old, the rich and poor, and the wise and simple all play host to fear at some time in their life. Some fears are absurd and ridiculous, having life only in the imagination. Others are very real such as losing work, of experiencing failure or growing older and struggling with illness and death. The range of fears visited upon us and the variety of forms it assumes is astounding. Imagined or real, fears sap our energy and vitality, leaving us helpless and hopeless. What are we to do with our fears? Jesus, on the night he was betrayed, struggled with fear. His response provides guidance for meeting and managing this crippling experience.

Jesus' initial response is to acknowledge his fear. Asking that "this cup of suffering" be removed is an honest appraisal of his fear. He identifies the presence of fear and looks squarely at it. Jesus' practice suggests that it is a mistake to take no account of fear or to repress it or to bottle it up. In fact, many psychologists agree that an attempt to drive fears from the mind establishes the fear more and more into our subconscious where it festers, and the crippling power is increased. Jesus does not bluff himself or others. He is afraid, and he shares that fear freely with his disciples and his heavenly Father. Truthful acknowledgement of fears that grasp us is not weakness but wisdom.

The second lesson Jesus offers is to acknowledge that fears are driven by the desire for self-preservation. Basic survival is primitive and instinctive. It is how any species – including humans – have endured threats that continually confront life. We all want health, joy, and the assurance of security. If there is one thing that we are afraid of more than any other fear, it is the fear that these things may be snatched from us. Jesus is no exception. Here, in the garden that fretful night, Jesus wishes that suffering might be removed from him. At its core, fears demonstrate that we are very much wrapped-up in ourselves.

We best manage our fears when we frankly acknowledge that we want to survive.

Third, Jesus directs us to take our fears to God in prayer, seeking to submit our basic desire for survival to a higher, and a more noble aspiration; the aspiration of pursuing God's will. Jesus never stated it more plainly than when he said, "All who want to come after me must say no to themselves… (Matthew 16:24)." Jesus is asking that we put God above all else, including our own desire to grasp life. In the proportion that we are able to do this, self-centeredness, the cause of so many fears, is diminished. When self-centeredness is diminished, so are our fears. We cannot decide what will happen to us. But we can decide what will happen in us – how we will respond to the fears that visit us. Jesus shows us the way.

Gracious God, your will for me is life and not death. Strengthen me when I am weak and grant me courage when I am afraid, in the sure confidence that you will never let go of me. Amen.

A Faith that Is Good and Pleasing

"Don't be conformed to the patterns of this world, but be transformed by the renewing of your minds so that you can figure out what God's will is – what is good and pleasing and mature."
Romans 12:2 (Common English Bible)

We are all too some extent suggestible. Stand still on the sidewalk and look up with enthralled interest and a crowd will quickly gather around staring upwards. The instinct to go along and do as others do is a powerful force. We are like clay, easily shaped and molded by our environment. It is a fact that those in the advertising industry count on. A product or service is presented as something that will enhance life, others testify to the veracity of the promises made and, in some measure, we are separated from our dollars – convinced of the value to purchase as others have. Every day the wind of conformity blows across our consciousness, urging us to go along, be like everyone else, purchase like everyone else and not stand out.

But "standing out" is precisely what Paul wants for us! Patterning our behavior after the behavior of others and conforming to the world deeply troubles the apostle Paul. Here, in his letter to the Christian Church in Rome, Paul makes an appeal that we not surrender to the world and what the world values. Naturally, there is safety and comfort in going along, submitting to the shaping influence of the culture. But what is safe and comfortable also hampers growth in Christ just as the lack of exercise hampers the development of strong bodies. A strong and mature faith is the goal of those who follow Jesus. This kind of faith – a faith that is good and pleasing to God – is produced from eyes that are fixed upon Christ.

Directing our gaze upon Jesus, and away from the world, is how we begin to organize our life around him. Rather than stand in the place of everyone else, Paul asks that we listen for the movement of the Holy Spirit, stand in its path and permit it to sweep over us in its onward rush. William Barclay offers a fresh hearing of Paul's words: "And do not shape your lives to meet the fleeting fashions of this world; but be transformed from it, by the renewal of your mind, until the very essence of your being is altered." Paul would have liked that translation: "the very essence of your being is altered!"

Far too many in the church today fail to have robust convictions. When persons in leadership speak and behave in a manner that is contrary to God, they either fail to recognize it or they are fearful of holding their leaders accountable. This is the result of an anemic faith. Going along and getting along is preferable to the cross of fidelity to Christ. Paul desires followers of Jesus Christ that have developed such strength of maturity that they step into the world, recognize disobedience to God and accept the challenge of the storm that will blow across their lives when they call those leaders back to God purposes. And when the gusty winds blow, and the storm grows fierce, the mature in faith will not be shaken. Strengthening them will be the very power of the risen Christ.

Give me a spirit that is tireless in running toward the goal of a mature faith, one that is good and pleasing to you, O God. Amen.

When We Need Help

"Finally, let's draw near to the throne of favor with confidence so that we can receive mercy and find grace when we need help."
Hebrews 4:16 (Common English Bible)

This is truly one of the great passages of the New Testament. In these few words we are reminded that Jesus is a source of tremendous power, the place we turn to when we need help. Jesus is not someone who is incapable of understanding and sympathizing with our struggles. Jesus struggled as we struggle, was tempted as we are tempted, and endured disappointment as we endure disappointment, without ever committing any sin. Jesus is full of sympathy for us because he fought, as we fight, on the battlefields of human life. There is remarkable authenticity in the sympathy Jesus has for us because he tasted the same bitterness of conflict and hateful evil forces that seek our defeat. Yet, unfailingly, Jesus emerged a victor. His strength is now our strength.

It must not be forgotten that Jesus won battle after battle by using the same spiritual resource that is open to us – the spiritual power that comes from God in regular prayer. Jesus engaged no unnatural means to gain victory that is denied to us, no private miracle reserved only for God's Son. He fought as we fight, standing where we stand, with the same resource that is placed in our hands – regular communion with God through prayer. Victory by any other means would have been of little value for ordinary people like us. The guidance Jesus offers us, and the encouragement we receive, is from someone who battled with no more than what is available to us.

It is well to remember that temptation is not sin. Jesus was tempted – perhaps the best-known moment is when he is on a mountain, with God, for forty days following his baptism. But Jesus did not sin. It is not sin to discover that in some unguarded moment an unkind word for another may come into our mind or an impulse wells-up inside us that isn't our best self. A downward pull to our lower nature is not sin. It is sin to yield, when a loose rein is given to evil desires. And while we learn from Jesus' example that temptation is not sin, we also learn from Jesus that temptation must drive us to our knees in prayer. Human strength and resolve to avoid sin is simply insufficient.

The Gospels speaks often of the deep sympathy of Jesus. Whenever he was in the presence of human suffering or those who had been marginalized by others, the compassion of Jesus was powerfully exhibited. His sympathy stretched out and welcomed Zacchaeus, a dishonest tax collector, a woman caught in adultery, and numerous people afflicted with mental, emotional and physical disabilities. People were lifted and redeemed by his love and friendship. Jesus' resurrection is a bold declaration that that same Jesus is present with us today, his sympathy continuing to stretch toward every one of us when we need help. And these few words from Hebrews remind us that Jesus sympathy – and strength – is sufficient.

Gracious God, as you strengthen Israel so many centuries ago, so strengthen me today that I may live faithfully, secure in your care. Amen.

When the Door Remains Closed

"Meanwhile, Peter remained outside, knocking at the gate."
Acts 12:16 (Common English Bible)

This is truly one of the great passages of the New Testament. In these few words we are reminded that Jesus is a source of tremendous power, the place we turn to when we need help. Jesus is not someone who is incapable of understanding and sympathizing with our struggles. Jesus struggled as we struggle, was tempted as we are tempted, and endured disappointment as we endure disappointment, without ever committing any sin. Jesus is full of sympathy for us because he fought, as we fight, on the battlefields of human life. There is remarkable authenticity in the sympathy Jesus has for us because he tasted the same bitterness of conflict and hateful evil forces that seek our defeat. Yet, unfailingly, Jesus emerged a victor. His strength is now our strength.

It must not be forgotten that Jesus won battle after battle by using the same spiritual resource that is open to us – the spiritual power that comes from God in regular prayer. Jesus engaged no unnatural means to gain victory that is denied to us, no private miracle reserved only for God's Son. He fought as we fight, standing where we stand, with the same resource that is placed in our hands – regular communion with God through prayer. Victory by any other means would have been of little value for ordinary people like us. The guidance Jesus offers us, and the encouragement we receive, is from someone who battled with no more than what is available to us.

It is well to remember that temptation is not sin. Jesus was tempted – perhaps the best known moment is when he is on a mountain, with God, for forty days following his baptism. But Jesus did not sin. It is not sin to discover that in some unguarded moment an unkind word for another may come into our mind or an impulse wells-up inside us that isn't our best self. A downward pull to our lower nature is not sin. It is sin to yield, when a loose rein is given to evil desires. And while we learn from Jesus' example that temptation is not sin, we also learn from Jesus that temptation must drive us to our knees in prayer. Human strength and resolve to avoid sin is simply insufficient.

The Gospels speaks often of the deep sympathy of Jesus. Whenever he was in the presence of human suffering or those who had been marginalized by others, the compassion of Jesus was powerfully exhibited. His sympathy stretched out and welcomed Zacchaeus, a dishonest tax collector, a woman caught in adultery, and numerous people afflicted with mental, emotional and physical disabilities. People were lifted and redeemed by his love and friendship. Jesus' resurrection is a bold declaration that that same Jesus is present with us today, his sympathy continuing to stretch toward every one of us when we need help. And these few words from Hebrews remind us that Jesus sympathy – and strength – is sufficient.

I open my heart and my soul to your Spirit, O God, that I may receive again your encouragement and strength. Amen.

I Don't Remember Me (Before You)

"These things were my assets, but I wrote them off as a loss for the sake of Christ."
Philippians 3:7 (Common English Bible)

TJ and John Osborne, brothers, grew up playing music together in Deale, Maryland. Following their move to Nashville they joined together as a vocal duo to become Brothers Osborne. Their most recent album, Port Saint Joe includes a rather nostalgic track, I Don't Remember Me (Before You). Widely considered one of the deepest tracks on the album, the song speaks to the man who can't remember – or maybe doesn't want to remember – what his life was like before he met the love of his life: "I heard I was a wild one. I feel like a child, son. But I really don't recall." And a few lines later, "I've seen pictures. And I've heard stories 'bout the boy I used to be. But I don't remember me." The song is a bold declaration that once he fell in love with another he wanted to grow up and change his ways for the better. Now, looking back, he is unable to recognize the man he was before.

A similar tune plays in the Apostle Paul's letter to the Church in Philippi, the Book of Philippians. The letter is Paul's declaration of his love for Jesus Christ. Near the middle of this letter Paul recalls the man he used to be before Christ: a man of considerable stature in the Jewish faith, garnering wide respect from others for his faithful, and rigid, observance of the Jewish law – a Pharisee par excellence! More, Paul confesses to being somewhat of a braggart, "With respect to righteousness under the Law, I'm blameless." (Verse 3:6b) Unlike the man in the Brothers Osborne track, Paul remembers his former self with great clarity. But then everything changed for Paul. He fell in love with Jesus. Now Paul looks back upon who he was before Jesus entered his life and determines that he was a foolish man – a man that valued the wrong things. What Paul once regarded as assets are now written off as a loss.

It is important for Paul to share with his readers his credentials before becoming a follower of Jesus. His resume sparkles and he dares anyone to present credentials that are more impressive. Paul doesn't embrace Jesus as someone who had nothing – or nothing to lose. Through the optics of what the world regards as of great value, Paul had it all. Paul had built an enviable life and reputation. Paul held "assets" that other people only dreamed of having. In possession of all anyone could have wanted Paul is invited into a relationship with Jesus. Now Paul has discovered the superior value of knowing Christ Jesus as Lord. What he once considered assets no longer has any value. Paul's point could not be clearer. The reader is in possession of nothing that is of more value than knowing Jesus.

Brothers Osborne song begins with the question, "Did I stop and watch the sunset fade? What gave me life and took my breath away?" These are questions that diminishes the value of a life lived before falling in love. TJ and John Osborne advance that very point later in the song, "Was my heart beatin' in my chest? Was I even alive?" Paul confesses to as much in his letter to the Church in Philippi, "In Christ I have a righteousness that is not my own and that does not come from the Law but rather from the faithfulness of Christ." (Verse 3:9) Before Christ, all Paul thought he possessed had been simply an illusion. Now Paul sings another tune, "I've heard stories 'bout the boy I used to be. But that was before you, before you."

Lord Jesus, give me the grace to behold your glory and recognize that without you, I possess nothing. Amen.

Don't Complain!

"The whole Israelite community complained against Moses and Aaron in the desert. 'Who are we? Your complaints aren't against us but against the Lord.'"
Exodus 16:2, 8b (Common English Bible)

Lowell Russell, formerly Executive Secretary and Director of the National Presbyterian Church and Center, Washington, D.C., once shared a lesson he learned from an attorney – a series of propositions that the attorney had written down on paper and kept with him at all times. There were three: "Never tell anyone how much you have to do. Never speak of your problems, your difficulties. Never talk about your disappointments." In other words, he was saying to himself, "Don't complain!"[18]

My friend and mentor, Arthur Caliandro, who followed Norman Vincent Peale as the senior pastor of Marble Collegiate Church in New York City, once shared with me his conviction that every pastor would be wise to preach on forgiveness at least three times a year. Caliandro believed that the single greatest obstacle to obtaining full Christian maturity was our difficulty with forgiveness. Any failure to forgive results in a weight that must be carried – by both the injured and the one who caused the injury. For Caliandro, the greatest burden was carried by the one who failed to forgive. Over time, the accumulation of "transgressions" that remain unforgiven results in stagnation of our spiritual growth. Christian growth isn't possible without the extravagant practice of forgiveness as Christ forgives us.

Perhaps my friend is correct. Yet, I contend that another hindrance to our growth as Christians is our propensity to complain. Here, in the Book of Exodus, the whole Israelite community complained against Moses and Aaron in the desert. Food was scarce, the days in the desert were hot and the journey through the desert seemed as though it would never end. Life back in Egypt as slaves seemed to present a better quality of life than a trek through the desert! So, the whole Israelite community complained.

Moses and Aaron's response seems to suggest the uselessness of negative thinking and speaking. Yes, the days in the desert were difficult. Discouragement is to be expected. But time and energy "moaning and groaning" provided no relief. So Moses and Aaron deflected the complaints; redirected the complaints made against them to God. It was the exercise of extraordinary leadership. That is because it forced upon the Israelite people the absolute necessity to pay attention to God, to "make their complaint" before God and then "to listen" for how God would respond. It is then that Moses and Aaron fulfilled their primary call to spiritual leadership – beginning the conversation between God's people and God. That is where spiritual growth occurs.

Thank you, O Lord, for your abiding presence in my life. Strengthen and support me in those moments I become discouraged and the way becomes difficult. Amen.

---

[18]Lowell Russell, "The Hard Rut of Complaining," *Best Sermons, Volume X*. (New York: Trident Press, 1968), 79.

Living with Tension

"Therefore, stop worrying about tomorrow, because tomorrow will worry about itself. Each day has enough trouble of its own."
Matthew 6:34 (Common English Bible)

A more promising title for this meditation might be: *Living Without Tension*. Yet, that is a promise that is neither realistic nor supported by the Bible. Mark's Gospel declares that on the night of Jesus' arrest, Jesus "began to feel despair and was anxious" (Mark 14:33). Amanda Enayati, writing for *Success* magazine asserts, "The greatest myth is that stress-free living exists at all. In reality the only time you are truly stress-free is when you are dead."[19] Yet, here in Jesus' Sermon on the Mountain, he seems to suggest that we have the capacity to "stop worrying."

Except, Jesus doesn't say that. Jesus teaches that we are to "stop worrying about tomorrow." There is a considerable difference. It is unlikely that any one of us can simply shut-off any concern or worry. What Jesus offers is the possibility of limiting our worry to one day at a time. As Jesus points out, "Each day has enough trouble of its own."

What has been observed over and over again by psychologists is that women and men become tired, run-down and discouraged not by the challenges that confront them today. What drains our energy is our frightened concern over what waits for us on the horizon – what we have to do tomorrow, and the day after that. This doesn't mean that we don't prepare for tomorrow. It simply means that we don't work ourselves up into an anxious knot and fever of apprehension worrying about tomorrow. Today, teaches Jesus, is enough to be concerned about.

What are we to do? All that Jesus had to say about living is fixed firmly on belief and trust in God. God is in our future – we are not left to it alone. The night of Jesus' arrest was filled with tension and worry. But do not fail to notice what Jesus does with it all. Jesus prays. Jesus claims the presence and concern of a living God that restored his energy and brought healing. What Jesus asks is that we do the same. Do our best today and leave the rest to God. This is a truth that we can accept because it comes from Christ. It is first and last the secret of victorious living.

Gracious God, increase my trust in your care and help me live a calm and tranquil life that Christ may be seen in me. Amen.

---
[19] Amanda Enayati, "Dissection Stress." *Success.* December 2015, pages 48-51.

Dear Hate

"God is love, and those who remain in love remain in God and God remains in them."
1 John 4:16b (Common English Bible)

Dear Hate is a deeply moving song, written as an epistolary conversation with hared itself, introducing hate as a character "on the news today" and having the capacity to "poison any mind." Written by Maren Morris, Tom Douglas and David Hodges and performed by Morris and Vince Gill, the song pinpoints the garden – presumably the Garden of Eden from the pages of Genesis – as hate's origin. The voices of Morris and Gill, supported only by two acoustic guitars, lead the listener along a serpentine path from Selma, Alabama ("you were smiling from that Selma bridge"), to Dallas, Texas ("when that bullet hit and Jackie cried"), culminating in New York City ("You pulled those towers from the sky"). Yet, hope remains, "But even on our darkest nights, the world keeps spinning 'round."

Hatred's power, made visible, is answered three times by a confident affirmation, "love's gonna conquer all." It is then that the last chorus flips the narrative of hatred's destructive ambitions to address love as someone who is personal and omnipresent. Though doubt is identified, "Just when I think you've given up," the presence of love becomes unmistakable once again, "You were there in the garden when I ran from your voice. I hear you every morning through the chaos and the noise. You still whisper down through history and echo through these halls." Love then speaks, "love's gonna conquer all."

Here in 1 John, love's name is revealed, "God is love." More, a promise is made. Anyone who clings to love, not as a feeling but as intentional conduct towards others, will discover that they are, in fact, taking-up residence in God and God in them. It is precisely the demonstration of love toward one another, in obedience to Jesus' example and command, that the reassurance of love's power over hate becomes unquestioned. By the intentional and active force of love, given freely to others, Christians are able to abide in God and God in them, in a state of mutual indwelling. And it is precisely by this mutual indwelling that we know we are loved and that the very best that hate can summon will not defeat us.

Dear Hate stands among a growing canon of songs that grapple with hatred – most notably for this writer, Tim McGraw's Grammy-winning, "Humble and Kind" – and offers a heartening message that love is stronger. Most days, it seems, the news swings the camera toward another appearance of hatred, moving among us at its foulest. All of us fight back tears and struggle with doubt. It is precisely at those moments that Maren Morris and Vince Gill seeks to encourage us with the good news, "love's gonna conquer all. Gonna conquer all."

O God, it is easy to read the Bible and belong to the church. It is more difficult to love, particularly those I disagree with or those who have hurt me. Walk with me and mold my heart to love everyone as you love me. Amen.

The Trouble with Pessimists

"At that the boy's father cried out, 'I have faith; help my lack of faith.'"
Mark 9:23 (Common English Bible)

Here is a remarkable story of a man with remarkable candor and honesty before Jesus, "I have faith; help my lack of faith." The man has faith, but that faith seems to be running low like a car's gas tank that is not quite empty but requiring a stop at a gas station nonetheless. The man's son is ill. He has tried every avenue of hope, sought everyone for help, including Jesus' disciples. No one has been able to do anything for the boy. The boy remains with his illness. Calling from a crowd that had gathered around Jesus, the man asks Jesus, "If you can do anything, help us! Show us compassion!" (Mark 9: 22b CEB) It is a plea that shows evidence of life's failures and frustrations. Repeated disappointments in securing healing for his son has sapped the man's reserve of faith, of his capacity to hold onto hope.

As faith for this man wanes, nearly being dowsed by negative experiences, pessimism grows; "If you can do anything…" What is clear in this biblical narrative is that when faith diminishes, a void isn't what remains. As faith is depleted, pessimism enlarges to fill the space. Simply, a person either lives with a narrative that with God all things are possible, or they question the existence and activity of God. Life is lived with faith or with pessimism – or something between the two. This man is moving from the former to the latter. The concern for this man is that pessimism is growing rapidly as faith is withering. Pessimists are not people who don't believe. They are people who believe in the wrong thing. The denial of God and God's capacity to change our lives is every bit a belief structure.

Perhaps what is most remarkable about this story is that the man recognizes within himself the withering of faith and the flourishing of pessimism, "Help my lack of faith." He wants to turn things around in his belief narrative. Yet, he can't do it alone. When personal faith has reached its limits, the man throws himself on the grace of God. The man asks God to supply what the man cannot, a faith that once again expands measure upon measure until pessimism is choked-out. He is unwilling to concede to the growth of pessimism.

This man becomes our example. Repeated disappointments and difficulties can culminate in the unfortunate experience of believing in the wrong thing; of believing that life has no purpose and that we are victims of circumstance, some of it good and some that results in pain and loss. This remarkable story is a call to not settle when life disappoints. There is pain and failure and brokenness enough for all people to experience from time to time. But God remains God. The man in this story, from Mark's Gospel, grabs hold of whatever faith he has that remains and clings to God, trusting that it will be enough. And it is.

Help me build a foundation of faith that sustains me in all of life. Amen.

How to Know God Better

"...growing in the knowledge of God."
Colossians 1:10 (Common English Bible)

John Leith, theologian and teacher of the faith, once told me in a personal conversation, that the single greatest threat to the vitality of the Christian church is amnesia – the failure of the typical church member to remember the most rudimentary content of the Bible. Increasingly, those who self-identify as followers of Jesus Christ have no intentional and regular plan for reading the Old and New Testament. Yet, there remains no substitute for strengthening our grip of spiritual matters and personally contributing to a fresh and robust witness of the Christian faith. The Bible must be read regularly by God's people for spiritual transformation.

Growth in the knowledge of God always begins with stillness. That is one of the non-negotiable conditions of knowledge of any subject. Stillness, as modeled by Jesus, is not necessarily the opposite of noise and tumult, though neither contributes to thoughtful reflection. Rather, stillness is slowing down, withdrawing from the routine of life, and turning one's focus to one thing. The four gospels record Jesus regularly "withdrawing" from his disciples and other people to turn his attention to God alone. If we want to know more of God – indeed, to know God better – we must relax the strain of constant daily demands that are placed upon us and read God's word.

Experiencing God deeply, as a reality in our lives, increases as we read the biblical witness of God's mighty acts upon God's people. Through the pages of scripture, we hear God whispering, "I am with you!" But there is more. As we penetrate the stories of the Bible and listen to their claim upon us, we also hear an invitation: "Are you willing to be with me; to live into a relationship with me?" The biblical witness is always calling to us, imploring us to turn away from choices that ultimately result in our disappointment, injury or death. Attention to God in the pages of the Bible impacts the decisions we make each day. Measure upon measure we discover that we not only know God better. Our lives are changed.

As we enter the unsearchable riches of God, in the pages of the Bible, our growth in the knowledge of God becomes as organic and natural as the growth of a seed planted in rich, fertile soil. Growth is a mysterious process that belongs to God. Our responsibility, as with the planting of seed in the ground, is to provide the necessary nurture – the daily watering of the seed until we see the growth and eventual maturity of what was planted. Daily placing ourselves before God's word in a time of stillness is God's method for experiencing larger and larger growth in the knowledge of God. The witness and vitality of the church once known by a previous generation can happen again. It begins when the people of God recover the urgency to immerse themselves in the knowledge of God from reading the Bible.

Mighty God, equip me and change me by your Holy Word that my thoughts and actions are consistent with my claim to be a follower of Jesus Christ. Amen.

The Missing Factor in Our Faith

"This has happened because of the Lord; it is astounding in our sight!"
Psalm 118:23 (Common English Bible)

Many who occupy a seat in Sunday's worship have a reduced faith. They have given intellectual consent to the Christian ideas that they have received, either from their family, a loved one, or the persuasive witness of another. Perhaps they concur that the Christian church is a useful, necessary institution for the general wellbeing of a community and should be supported. Some may vigorously advance the argument that the world would be a better place if more people embraced basic Christian values. Yet, many of these same people would be immensely surprised if they ever caught God doing anything. The God of their faith is one who sits in heaven and does nothing. Expectancy of God actually moving and working powerfully in the world is the missing factor of their faith.

Not so with the writer of these few words from the Psalms. Doubtless, this writer believes that God acts in the world. What we know is that something happened, that God seems to be the only explanation, and that it was astounding. No longer is God a mere object of belief, God is someone to be experienced; experienced as a force operative in the world. We are not told what happened. What we do know is that it changed this persons' whole complexion of faith. This vital sense of the reality of God – and God's activity in the world – presents a striking contrast with much of the faith that is common today.

Some years ago, a popular television program, The A-Team, developed a fictional narrative of four Vietnam vets, framed for a crime they didn't commit. Each weekly episode featured an elaborate – an unlikely – collaboration of the four helping the innocent while on the run from the military. Following the always heroic and successful effort of the four to correct an injustice, Col. John "Hannibal" Smith, the leader of the team, would lean back with a lit cigar, smile, and say, "I love it when a plan comes together!" That must have been the experience of the Psalmist when something always believed in suddenly works. There was a present difficulty, and God showed-up!

Of course, astounding things are supposed to happen. We are not alone in the world, watched over by a disinterested God seated in heaven. Whatever else God may be, the Bible is clear that God is a spiritual force waiting to be released through the lives of those who believe, who are expectant of God's activity, and are daily aligning their lives with the teachings of Jesus Christ. Perhaps nothing is more profoundly absurd than the Christian who professes belief in a great God but fails to expect astounding results from that belief. The Psalmist experience can be our own. It begins with expectant prayer, eyes wide-open for the astounding things God will do with us and through us.

Open the windows of my heart to new expectations of your astounding work in my life. Amen.

Getting Started with Jesus

"Everybody who hears these words of mine and puts them into practice is like a wise builder who built a house on bedrock."
Matthew 7:24 (Common English Bible)

How does a person start to be a Christian? For many in the church, it is a startling question. It is startling because so little thought has been given to the question. Christianity has been reduced to joining a church, worshipping on Sunday morning when convenient, faithfully completing a financial pledge card once a year, and an occasional appearance at a congregational dinner. The notion that there is anything more escapes them. What also escapes such people is any vital relationship with Jesus Christ. And a vital relationship with Jesus will remain absent until behind every conventional practice of faith a person goes directly to Jesus, listens to the teachings of Jesus, and puts those teachings into practice in their own life. A person gets started with being a Christian by endeavoring to live as Christ lived.

Simply, being a Christian is something to be done. Christianity is not consent to a particular theological creed, belonging to a church that self-identifies as Christian, or practicing a set of rituals. Christianity is doing what Christ does. In every account of Jesus calling particular men to be his disciples something is absent; what is absent is a requirement of a theological education, or a seminar on the basics of the faith, or a new member class. The only thing that Jesus asks is, "Will you follow me?" We will never understand everything that the church teaches. And there may be some teachings that we understand but we simply cannot believe. Jesus doesn't ask for either. Yesterday, and today, Jesus asks one thing: "Will you follow me?"

In the second place, though we begin where we are – with little understanding of Jesus or no understanding of Jesus – we do not remain where we are. Following Jesus is a continuous journey of listening to all that Jesus teaches and appropriating what is understood into the daily practice of life. As this is done, each week, each month, and each year brings clearer insight and a deeper assurance of Christ's presence and strength for our lives. Faith matures as the season changes from spring, to summer, to fall, to winter, and finally back to spring with all the new growth each new spring brings. As we pay increasing attention to Jesus, learn more from him, and think harder how to walk as Jesus walked, we make progress toward a more confident faith.

Getting started with Jesus is not difficult. Remaining on the walk will be one of the most difficult challenges of life. That is because of all the distractions and temptations to walk a different path, a path that promises quicker satisfactions and pleasures. But what God already knows – and what many of us discover by our own experience – is that every other path ends with disappointment and loss. But strength is available to those who wish to remain on the path of Jesus. That strength is found in the daily reading of the Bible, regular prayer, and the use of helpful devotional material prepared by trusted followers of Jesus Christ. By these resources our confidence in God, in Jesus Christ, and the available help of the Holy Spirit grows upon us.

I know what you require, O God. Guide my steps today and all my tomorrows as I try to live as your Son, Jesus. Amen.

Space Cowboy

"I call heaven and earth as my witnesses against you right now: I have set life and death, blessing and curse before you. Now choose life - so that you and your descendants will live – by loving the Lord your God, by obeying his voice, and by clinging to him."
Deuteronomy 30:19, 20a (Common English Bible)

Occasionally I hear a song on the radio that is so raw, direct, and reflective that it grasps my heart and simply will not let go. Kacey Musgraves' song, *Space Cowboy*, is the most recent addition to that canon of songs. Only two weeks ago did I hear this beautiful and haunting song on the radio and found that I was bound – heart, soul, and mind – by its lyrics. It simply would not let me go and I had not the slightest clue why. The basic narrative of the song is about finally letting go of a dying relationship and the deep sorrow that follows. Though heartbreak is deeply and powerfully infused in the lyrics, that narrative is not my narrative. In a few weeks I will celebrate thirty-one years of marriage and I have never stopped adoring my wife and finding imaginative ways of expressing my love for her.

What was inevitable for me was the decision to download this song onto my iPhone and listen to it again and again, not understanding the inescapable hold it had on my imagination. This morning, during my morning run – and listening to this song again and again on the "repeat" mode – the mist of confusion scattered and with piercing clarity heard what my subconscious had heard all along: Musgraves' words have become God's word to me, "You look out the window while I look at you." Several weeks ago, I turned fifty-eight, and that birthday gave me pause to ponder just how much of my life has been frittered away looking "out the window," longing for something more.

It is difficult to appreciate and value a blessing you are standing right in the middle of when your gaze is out the window, wanting something else. And the whole time my focus is out that window, God's focus is right on me, longing that I not let go of God's claim on me; not letting go of God's deep love for me. It is true that in my baptism I attached myself to God's redemptive work in the world. But fundamentally, God demands less of me than what God desires to give me. But God's gifts are inextricably bound to "obeying his voice, and by clinging to him." Yet, God will not "close the gate" and "fence me in." God sets before each of us the choice to "cling" to a deeply satisfying relationship with God or to pursue whatever it is we see out the window.

Rarely do I watch the video of songs I enjoy. Nancy Fine, my colleague in ministry, suggested to me this morning that I watch this video. The final scene is the clincher for me: as the lyrics repeat, "You can have your space, cowboy. I ain't gonna fence you in. Go on, ride away in your Silverado" the young cowboy in question rides away. Musgraves is bathed in the soft light of the remaining light of dusk while dark clouds appear and close-in all around the one who chooses to leave. The implication is clear: what is "out the window" lacks the beauty of what is left behind. Here, in these words from Deuteronomy, God already knows that and pleas with us, "Choose life, choose me, choose us."

Thank you, God, for the blessings of my life. Order my steps this day that I might walk more closely with you. Amen.

God's Purpose. God's Call. God's Power

"...so is my word that comes from my mouth; it does not return to me empty. Instead, it does what I want, and accomplishes what I intend."
Isaiah 55:11 (Common English Bible)

Reading the Bible, with a fresh and alert mind, impacts and stirs the reader in extraordinary and often unanticipated ways. Because the printed words belong to a real, present, and active God, the words are used imaginatively and purposefully, in a tailored fashion, for each individual reader. Reading the Bible is never a solo activity. God, in the Holy Spirit, is always present, accomplishing a purposeful work in the mind and heart of the individual who comes expectant to experience something new. When the mind is dull and expects little from reading the Bible, this dynamic and amazing power is absent. In my own engagement with the Bible each morning, I experience three reoccurring themes.

First, the Bible reveals the purposefulness of God. Perhaps in no other place in scripture is this more clearly and directly presented than in the twelfth chapter of Genesis, verses 1-3: God promises to bless Abraham. But, with penetrating clarity, this blessing is ultimately for the purpose of blessing all of humanity. A blessing to all people, of all nations, is the bottom line of God's promise to Abraham. God's unfolding purpose may be too vast and, at times, imperceptible, to be grasped this side of the grave, but, at least, we are assured by the Bible that the world has been delivered from meaninglessness. With this knowledge, we can live quietly and confidently, trusting the care of the future to God.

Second, the Bible reveals God's call upon each person. Assuming a robust theological posture, the Apostle Paul declares in Ephesians 2:10 that we were, "...created in Christ Jesus to do good things. God planned for these good things to be the way that we live our lives." Candidly, Paul corrects the notion that followers of Jesus Christ are to participate, here and there, in good work. No; good work, or doing good things, is to be our way of life. It is all part of God's divine activity that our own lives be caught-up in the one grand purpose that God is continually unfolding in the world. Each person's life is made integral to God's resolve to gather the nations under the Lordship of his Son, Jesus Christ.

Third, the Bible reveals God's power. God is not defeated. With panoramic vision, Paul captures the human condition in Romans 8: "Who will separate us from Christ's love? Will we be separated by trouble, or distress, or harassment, or famine, or nakedness, or danger, or sword? As it is written, we are being put to death all day long for your sake. We are treated like sheep for slaughter. But in all these things we win a sweeping victory through the one who loved us." (Verses 35-37 CEB) Contrary to appearances, difficulties, hardships, and death will not defeat God and those who belong to God. Struggle will certainly manifest itself in every life. But at the end we will discover that our life has been guided and loved, and that disaster is over-ruled. More, we will find that nothing of value is lost.

God, make me alert to your purpose, you call upon me that I may be useful to you, and grant me a fresh encounter of your power at work in the world. Amen.

When God Seems Distant

"I'm convinced that nothing can separate us from God's love in Christ Jesus our Lord."
Romans 8:38a (Common English Bible)

Tommy Lasorda, former manager of the Los Angeles Dodgers, tells about an experience he had in church. One Sunday he was in Cincinnati for a ball game against the Reds. That morning he went to early morning Mass and happened to see the Red's manger there. They were old friends and sat beside each other during Mass. Afterward, the Red's manager said, "Tommy, I'll see you at the ballpark. I'm going to hang around a little." Lasorda said that when he reached the door, he glanced back over his shoulder. He noticed that his friend was praying at the altar and lighting a candle. He said, "I thought about that for a few moments. Then, since we needed a win very badly, I doubled back and blew out his candle."[20] Though misguided, what a powerful demonstration of faith in God's presence and activity!

Countless people today long for that deep confidence in God's presence and activity in their lives. God seems distant to them. They plod through each day, fearful, anxious, and burdened with uncertainty. Some may remember once having a close relationship with God but that was a long time ago. Prayers seem to never rise higher than the ceiling – and that is when we even feel like praying! The good news is that this is not an uncommon experience in the Christian faith. Just as people can grow apart in relationships with one another, so we can drift away from God. As Thomas Tewell once said to me, the difference is that in human relationships, both parties contribute to the distance. But, in a relationship with God, the reality is that we drift away from God. God never drifts away from us.

In those moments when God seems distant, what are we to do? Perhaps an experience I had this past week will help. My daughter, Rachael, is in Norway – a studio photographer for the Holland America Cruise Lines. It's not uncommon for Rachael to work twelve- and fourteen-hour days. Wi-Fi is limited and with her long hours it is difficult to "connect" with her by telephone or by other means in real time. Just this week, Rachael reached-out to me via Facebook Messenger. She said that for a limited time she was available to receive a phone call from me and that she really would like me to call. Immediately, I moved something that was already on my calendar to another time and placed the call. Do you see what happened? Suddenly, my greatest desire was to speak with my daughter. To do so, I had to make the time.

We reconnect with God the same way. We move beyond our desire to be close with God and carve-out time from our busy lives to simply be still in God's presence. We open the Bible and read expectantly, asking God to speak powerfully through the words that we read on the page. We learn from our reading more about God, about God's good desires for us, and we learn what God requires of us. We spend time together with God. And we listen; we listen deeply in the silence following our reading to the hunches, the promptings, and the direction we sense from God. As we respond positively, the distance we once felt from God begins to close.

Thank you, O God, for your love that continuously surrounds me. Amen.

---

[20]William R. Bouknight, *The Authoritative Word: Preaching Truth in A Skeptical Age.* (Nashville: Abingdon Press, 2001) 30.

Unnamed Saints

"But his disciples took him by night and lowered him in a basket through an opening in the city wall."
Acts 9:25 (Common English Bible)

On March 4th, 1921 the United States Congress approved the burial of an unidentified American serviceman from World War I in the Arlington National Cemetery in Virginia. Today, that monument is known as the Tomb of the Unknown Soldier. It is considered one of the highest honors to serve as a Sentinel at the Tomb – fewer than 20 percent of all volunteers are accepted for training and of those only a fraction pass training to become Tomb Guards. Out of respect for the interred, the sentinels command silence at the tomb from the thousands who visit each year. Inscribed on the Western panel: Here Rests in Honored Glory an American Soldier Known but To God.

The Apostle Paul is the greatest evangelist of the early Christian Church and author of nearly two-thirds of the New Testament. Soon following his conversion to that faith, he once sought to extinguish from the religious landscape, the Jews and their leaders at Damascus sought to silence him. In fact, Acts narrates that "the Jews hatched a plot to kill Saul (Paul's former name)" and, "They were keeping watch at the city gates around the clock, so they could assassinate him." Paul escaped by the heroic act of unnamed disciples who, "took him by night and lowered him in a basket through an opening in the city wall."

Not one of the disciples who aided in Paul's escape is named. Their identity remains unknown. Yet, each one played an important part in the history of the Apostle Paul, without whom, Paul's great work might have never been completed. Paul would go forward from that glorious night to cover thousands of miles by sea and by land preaching the resurrection of Jesus Christ. Churches would be planted and life after life would be changed by his message of hope and eternal life available in the name of Jesus. Through the robust ministry of the Apostle Paul, the Holy Spirit gave birth to a movement that would change the world. Yet, without the loyalty and devotion and courage of a few unnamed disciples one particular night, Paul would have perished at the hands of his enemies in Damascus.

Our nation remains grateful to the tremendous leadership of great leaders such as General Patton, General Eisenhower, and General MacArthur. The Christian Church continues to build upon the work of the Apostle Paul that is without parallel. But it is true in our nation's history and the history of the church that who they were and what they contributed would have never been realized had it not been for the loyalty, devotion, and courage of the unknown soldiers and unnamed saints who risked their lives, and in many cases laid down their lives for something they believed in. We all depend upon one another. We all need each other. And nothing becomes strong without the strength of the many.

Lord Jesus Christ, you come to us in the midst of our brokenness, claim us as your own, and equip us for good work. Bless our hands, and the work we do, that lives may be changed by your power. Amen.

Figuring Out God's Will

"Don't be conformed to the patterns of this world but be transformed by the renewing of your minds so that you can figure out what God's will is – what is good and pleasing and mature."
Romans 12:2 (Common English Bible)

Antoine de Saint-Exupery wisely said, "A goal without a plan is just a wish." It is ludicrous to suggest that any follower of Jesus lacks the goal of spiritual growth; lacks the desire to become more Christlike than they are presently. Adult baptism and membership in a church are intentional decisions. No one stumbles into the Christian faith. And ask anyone seated in church on Sunday morning if they would like to be a better Christian and I doubt there will be any surprises. There is really only one reasonable answer. Ask that question and I imagine you may receive some strange looks. Common courtesy may prevent an honest answer but stirring in the minds of many would be the curt response, "Do you know the trouble I had this morning to simply show-up at church?" No one stumbles into the Christian faith. And no one stumbles into Christian worship. Naturally, every follower of Jesus has the goal of spiritual maturity.

The difficulty is that in many faith communities, in many churches, there is so little evidence of Christian growth. Listen carefully to many church members and they sound no different than those who remain outside the church doors. Gossip abounds, grumbling is heard and self-righteous judgement is whispered in every pew. Perhaps each person guilty of such bad behavior desires to be better than this but there is simply no movement in that direction. The reason should haunt each of us. We lack an intentional plan for growth. Antoine de Saint-Exupery is correct, without a plan, the desire for becoming increasingly Christlike is nothing more than a wish. Worse, without a plan for growth, says Paul, the natural consequence is conformity to the patterns of the world.

If a wish is ever to become a goal, a plan is required. Weight Watchers offers a plan if the goal is to lose weight. Fitness Centers offer a plan if the goal is improved fitness and health. Language video and audio programs may be purchased if the goal is learning a new language. Any goal must be translated into a plan or it simply remains a wish. The same principal applies to spiritual growth. The plan need not be difficult or complex. In fact, the likelihood that a plan will be placed into action increases if it is simple to understand and follow.

Paul's words here offer a glorious promise. Identify a spiritual growth plan, remove it from the box and implement it fully and the result will be growing clarity of God's will. Some people despair because God's will is often difficult to know. Many times that is because they expect clarity without effort, without following an intentional plan for growth. The trouble is that God's will for our lives is always inextricably bound to a growing relationship with God. It is never one or the other. Pursue an ongoing relationship with God and God's desires will become apparent.

Our Heavenly Father, we give you thanks for the amazing power available to us in your promises. Help us to be wise enough to claim this power by intentionally pursuing a daily relationship with you. Amen.

Happy People

*"From now on, brothers and sisters, if anything is excellent
and if anything is admirable, focus your thoughts on these things:
all that is true, all that is holy, all that is just,
all that is pure, all that is lovely, and all that is worthy of praise."*
Philippians 4:8 (Common English Bible)

Happy People, a song recorded by the country group Little Big Town, features positive lyrics that both evoke feelings of joy and well-being as it encourages kindness and a positive approach to daily life: "Happy people don't cheat. Happy people don't lie. They don't judge, or hold a grudge, don't criticize." Supported by a driving percussion rhythm, the memorable lyrics sound a poignant note of the choices each of us are called to make daily – the choice to collapse beneath the hurt and brokenness that may come our way or the choice to rise above the fray of disappointment and positively move forward as best we can, "Here's to whatever puts a smile on your face. Whatever makes you happy people."

These lyrics offer sound counsel for living. It is the same counsel offered by the apostle Paul to those living in Philippi, "…if anything is excellent and if anything is admirable, focus your thoughts on these things." Paul does not address the external circumstances the people may be facing. In fact, those external circumstances are very difficult. There is a constant threat of persecution for their faith and quarrels among the spiritual leaders of the church are tearing at the fabric of their community. Yet, these difficulties, though serious, are not to be determinative for the life of Christians. Followers of Jesus Christ do not "react" toward what is happening all around them – they "respond" positively, confident in the presence of the risen Christ working through them for the reconciliation of the world.

The difference between "reacting" and "responding" to daily life, and all each day brings, is considerable. Those who "react" give power to the circumstances of life for which they have little control. It is a power that will determine if the day will be filled with defeat or victory, sadness or happiness. The decision is made for us. But those who "respond" to daily life reserve that decision for themselves. For Christians, that decision is grounded in the certainty that, come what may each day, we belong to God. It is that knowledge that creates joy regardless of the circumstances we may find surrounding us.

Paul asks that we "focus" our thoughts. That is an intentional, purposeful decision, not a reactive one. Paul then proceeds to identify the qualities that are to occupy our minds and shape our character as a people of God: "all that is true, all that is holy, all that is just, all that is pure, all that is lovely, and all that is worthy of praise." We are reminded that the course of our life need not be directed by what happens to us but, rather, how we chose to face daily challenges. Little Big Town concludes their song, *Happy People*, "Well life is short. And love is rare. And we all deserve to be happy while we're here." Paul wants us to know that the decision is ours.

Sustain me with your word so that I may be your presence in this world, providing hope and encouragement to each person I meet. Amen.

Dear God

"I pleaded with the Lord three times for it to leave me alone. He said to me, 'My grace is enough for you, because power is made perfect in weakness.' So I'll gladly spend my time bragging about my weaknesses so that Christ's power can rest on me."
2 Corinthians 12:8, 9 (Common English Bible)

Someone once remarked that promised prayer has no power, only practiced prayer. Hunter Hayes practices powerful prayer in his single, *Dear God*. Written alongside pop singer Andy Grammer and Dave Spencer, the song is a prayer between Hunter and God as Hunter wrestles with faith and self-doubt: "Are you sure there's nothing wrong with me?" The song's theme of self-doubt is advanced almost immediately following that lyric with the raw, honest, and expressive line, "And why do I feel like I'm not enough? Dear God, are you sure that you don't mess up?" Here is a question that is asked all the time by people of faith – a valid and authentic question that presses in those moments of disappointment, failure, and pain.

A part of the human condition – and validated by experience – is the striving to live into a higher purpose and meaning in life. In those moments when we stumble and are made vulnerable by exposed weaknesses, the thought of feeling like "I'm not enough" unsettles us. This is precisely the experience of the apostle Paul in his words to the church in Corinth. Paul suffers from an unnamed affliction, what appears to be a chronic and debilitating problem. Paul's zeal to preach the Gospel of Jesus Christ is hampered by this affliction so Paul comes before God, in prayer, on three separate occasions asking that the affliction be removed. Anyone who has a struggle, infirmity, or difficulty accepts the reasonableness of Paul's request. Yet, Paul's request is denied.

What is apparent by any close reading of Paul's ministry – both before his conversion to Christ and following – is that he is a self-sufficient person. Paul is intelligent, resourceful, and driven. Such persons rarely need others, much less God. When a weakness becomes evident, such people develop a laser-like focus on conquering and prevailing over the weakness as they again move forward to greater success and accomplishments. Hunter acknowledges as much in his song, "The truth is it's not even you. It's just me that I'm up against." Hunter is dissatisfied with the frailty in his life: "Dear God, are you sure that you don't mess up?" Paul is no different. Paul is dissatisfied with the frailty in his life.

Paul's request for strength without weakness is refused. But Paul does receive a gift. Paul receives a deep understanding of the "riches" that are his in God's grace, "My grace is enough for you." As Paul must now embrace his weaknesses so also must he now embrace God's grace. The result is a stronger character, a deeper humility, and an uncommon ability to empathize with others. In the music video for the song, *Dear God*, Hunter is seen making his prayer to God through a flaring horn like those commonly seen on old phonograph devices. It makes perfect sense for anyone who has every pondered whether God hears our prayers. But God's refusal to remove Paul's limitations reminds each of us that, ultimately, God intends that we trust ourselves, and our future, to God's care.

Help me to be humble, as Jesus, who made himself nothing that through him the world may see your strength. Amen.

Hesitant Believers

"At that the boy's father cried out, 'I have faith; help my lack of faith!'"
Mark 9:24 (Common English Bible)

The boy's father cried out, "I have faith; help my lack of faith!" His cry is our cry. We live in an anxious time. Natural disasters, terrorist activity, and anger unleashed in the midst of shifting cultural values have brought uncertainty and fear. We may profess faith in God, but that faith is hesitant, uncertain, and unsatisfactory. The forces of evil, destruction, and pain can do that; diminish a steady and certain faith in the presence and activity of a loving God. Faith may remain, but it isn't the robust faith we desire. Mixed with our faith is a good measure of doubt: "help my lack of faith!"

This father's son is possessed with a destructive spirit. Since an early age, this spirit has thrown the boy into a fire and into bodies of water with one intention: to kill him. The Bible doesn't tell us how many years this has been going on, but the father has now exhausted all hope for his son. Hope extinguished is reflected in the father's question to Jesus: "If you can do anything." It is a frail request. It is what anyone who has nearly given-up would ask. In modern parlance, it is a resignation to, "What can it hurt to ask Jesus to help." The father has moved way past desperation.

It is then that the arch of the story shifts. Jesus confidently answers, "All things are possible for the one who has faith." The father finds that he stands before a faith so glorious and strong, a faith that has sufficient resources to meet any need, that his prayer grows larger. Certainly, the father's desire for his son's wholeness remains. But suddenly present is something more. The father seeks to possess the faith he sees in Jesus, "help my lack of faith!" How many of us are represented by that father's plea?

Each of us has felt the desire to find within our faith the resources to counterbalance the tumult of the world. These are desperate days we are living through. And as one tragedy follows another, we grow weary. Jesus does heal the father's son. And when the disciples ask how, Jesus simply answers, "Throwing this kind of spirit out requires prayer." Apparently, Jesus speaks of something more than perfunctory prayers offered before a meeting, a meal, or bedtime. If we wish to be glorious believers who call upon uncommon powers, we will fulfill the conditions of a more thoughtful, robust life of communion with God. This is a deeper prayer life than many of us have ever known.

There are days I struggle to be your child, O God; days that I struggle to be a faithful disciple of Jesus. Strengthen my faith when it is weak, hold me when I cannot walk, and remind me always that you hold my future in your loving embrace. Amen.

What Is Good

*"Only God is my rock and my salvation – my stronghold! –
I won't be shaken anymore."*
Psalm 62:2 (Common English Bible)

Captured in these few words is a powerful witness to abundant progress in our spiritual life: *"Only God is my rock and salvation – my stronghold! – I won't be shaken anymore."* The author of these words is contemplating difficult circumstances on the horizon. A storm is building in his personal life and a whirlwind is gathering strength and raging. Shortly, the author will be caught in the blast – in the very center of violence that is determined to destroy him. Yet, what is heard in these words is a faith that has moved from painful wobbling in a time of trouble to an experience of being unshakable; of standing strong in the work of the Lord: *"I won't be shaken anymore."*

A mood of fear and uncertainty is transformed. Present now is a voice of a more vital trust, and the suggestion of spiritual maturity. Where once he would have been shaken by the assault that was drawing near, he is now not overwhelmed. An unshaken confidence of a matured faith now occupies his heart and soul. What changed? He provides the answer – he has found a sturdy footing in the promises of God, *"my stronghold."* A trembling spirit that is placed into regular communion with God is settled; the timid fluttering of a heart is quieted. This is the calmness which comes from sharing in the strength of God; a strength that derives from intentional attention to relationship building with God.

When we nurture our own faith by attention to God's word and regular prayer, our relationship to God is deepened. In direct proportion to that deepening relationship we discover that fears are scattered and worries, once prolific, are diminished. Lives are no longer lived in small and frightened circles where the soul grows faint and timid. Attention to God, even in the ordinary moments of life, expands the chambers of our souls and our breath becomes deeper. Uncertainties of life become increasingly rare and our slipping feet are steadied upon a certain and firm foundation – *"only God is my rock."*

Here is the great secret of progress in our spiritual life – attentive and regular communion with God. Our own strength for meeting the trying and challenging circumstances of life is insufficient. Alone we will always be defeated. But we are not alone. These words from the Psalms are an invitation to put on the same strength and confidence of a life that cleaves to God. By God's strengthening fellowship we will face all the hostile forces of this world with ordered lives – lives which demonstrate to others the beauty of God's peace.

Gracious God, you neither faint or grow weary. Help me today to lean into you for strength when I feel powerless and to trust in your love for me when I am shaken. Amen.

Taking Jesus Seriously

"When Simon Peter saw the catch, he fell at Jesus' knees and said, 'Leave me, Lord, for I'm a sinner!'"
Luke 5:8 (Common English Bible)

Recently, I began working with a personal trainer after nearly five years of absence from a gym. Stepping into the gym I saw muscle tone where I lacked muscle tone. I saw the absence of fat where I had much. Here were women and men, of all ages, in nearly perfect physical form, radiant, confident, full of energy. I nearly turned and walked out the door. The comparison of these Olympian-like gods and goddesses to my aging, late 50's body disheartened me. Each person in the gym that morning disturbed me. I did not belong to this community. I cannot rise to that. Instinctively, I wanted to escape their company.

Luke's Gospel tells us that this was precisely Simon Peter's response when it dawned upon his consciousness who Jesus was, "…he (Peter) fell at Jesus' knees and said, 'Leave me, Lord, for I'm a sinner!'" Peter had come to know Jesus, welcomed Jesus as a guest in his home, and was welcomed by Jesus into discipleship. But, it was after Peter began to see the kind of person Jesus was, and the astonishing work Jesus did, that Peter realized – in both a stark and unsettlingly manner – that Peter stood in extraordinary company. Peter wasn't simply in the presence of a god-like individual. Peter was in the presence of God!

Simon Peter was right - right to understand so clearly and profoundly that satisfied admiration, adoration, and worship are insufficient in the reality of the divine presence of God. From the depths of Peter's whole being was released a cry, "Leave me, Lord." The divine presence disturbed Peter. He did not belong on that scale of life. Peter could not rise to that. Instinctively, Peter looked for an escape. Peter took Jesus seriously.

Many people have pretty much reduced their Christianity to an admiration of Jesus. Such a response is easy, and natural. Yet, that is all the Christianity they have – admiration. But that is not enough. To truly grasp the divine presence is unsettling. It is to become aware of just how far we are from that measure of life. And, unable to rise, we seek an escape. After approximately seven sessions with my personal trainer, Bill Dorton, he asked me to perform a chin-up. I could not. Not one. Again, I wanted to escape. And then Bill spoke, "I'll get you there." And it was enough to remain, struggling to become more. Jesus did the same for Peter, "Don't be afraid." It was Jesus promising Peter, "I'll get you there!" That day, Peter left everything and followed Jesus.

Surprising God, startle me with your presence this day that I may once again offer all of my life to you. Amen.

A Prescription for Living

"Love is patient, love is kind, it isn't jealous, it doesn't brag, it isn't arrogant, it isn't rude, it doesn't seek its own advantage, it isn't irritable, it doesn't keep a record of complaints, it isn't happy with injustice, but is happy with the truth."
1 Corinthians 13:4-6 (Common English Bible)

Earl Nightingale shares some wisdom for living he learned from Dr. Frederick Loomis who published an essay in 1949, "The Best Medicine."[21] Dr. Loomis wrote, "It's but little good you'll do, watering last year's crops. Yet that is exactly what I have seen hundreds of my patients doing in the past 25 years – watering with freely flowing tears things of the irrevocable past. Not the bittersweet memories of loved ones, which I could understand, but things done which should not have been done, and things left undone which should have been done." Dr. Loomis went on to write that one cannot live adequately in the present, nor effectively face the future, when one's thoughts are buried in the past. What must be done, insists Dr. Loomis, is to stop thinking about yourself – and how you have been hurt – and start thinking about other people.

This is precisely the teaching of the apostle Paul in these words he shares with the Christian community in Corinth, "(love) doesn't keep a record of complaints." We habitually think of love as a feeling or as an emotion. Yet, Paul shows no indication in 1 Corinthians 13 that love is to be understood in this fashion. For Paul, love is cognitive; it is a decision that produces behavior. Love – indeed the love demonstrated by Christ – always moves toward other people positively, seeking their welfare. Such love takes no notice of wrongs received by another. Rather, love sees the possibilities of changing people and moving all humanity toward the Kingdom that Christ embodied in himself.

Dr. Loomis writes that by the simple device of doing an outward, unselfish act today, each person can make the past recede; "The present and future will again take on their true challenge and perspective." He concludes his essay noting that, as a doctor, he has seen this approach being far more effective in changing lives than any prescription he could have ordered from the drugstore. As Earl Nightingale observes, those were the last words written by Dr.

Loomis, but they have kept him alive in the minds and actions of thousands, perhaps millions, of people who have chosen to test for themselves their practical value.

We all know people who nurse an injury, a slight or unkindness, perceived or real, they have received from another. Or, perhaps, they have suffered a tragedy in the past and simply cannot move past the hurt. They mull the memory over and over, keeping it fresh. What is done is done, and there is no remedy; no returning to the past to undo what was unpleasant. It is here that Dr. Loomis is very wise. The past cannot be changed but the present can. The course that is available, if one chooses, is to cease thinking about oneself and start thinking about others. Indeed, if we wish to destroy the envy, the anger and the evil that lurks in the world – and in our hearts – we refuse to react emotionally to the slights or harm done to us by others and respond with love. It is a prescription for living that we learn at the foot of the cross.

Turn my eyes from my past to opportunities to be of service to others today. Amen.

---

[21]Earl Nightingale, "A Prescription for Living," *Insight: A Time-Saving Source of New Ideas for Busy People* (Chicago: Nightingale-Conant Corporation, 1988) 5.

I Woke Up in Nashville

"Just like a deer that craves streams of water, my whole being craves you, God."
Psalm 42:1 (Common English Bible)

Country music artist, Seth Ennis, recently released what has been portrayed as a vulnerable love song, *I Woke Up in Nashville*. This piano-driven song builds a compelling story of a man, who leaves someone he loves for the promise of something more, presumably the bright lights of New York City. Convinced that everything he wanted was, "in this town," a pervasive emptiness overcomes him. There is a hole in his heart that the promises of the city cannot fill; a hole that will only be filled by the love he left in Nashville. The lights of New York, and the promises within them for a complete and joy filled life, fail him: "Cause those Broadway lights don't shine the way that your eyes did." The hollowness of life apart from Nashville drives him back to his first love and the longing for forgiveness; forgiveness that he ever left. Fugitively and literally, he wakes up back where he always belonged, in Nashville.

Here, the author of this Psalm is on the same journey. With the urgency of a deer, parched with thirst and seeking cool streams of water, the one who speaks in this Psalm craves God. It is a journey that we are familiar with. It is a timeless journey driven by an urge – the urge for God – that takes possession of the human heart. It is a journey that leaps across borders of races and nations and shows no regard for the boundaries of generations. Men and women chase after dreams, chase after the lights of Broadway, to discover that any dream that leaves God behind results in emptiness. In that moment when the Broadway lights dim before the remembrance of God's love, we rush back to Nashville; back to the embrace of God.

Although church membership and worship attendance is trending downward throughout the United States and Europe, considerable research reveals that there remains a deep and increasing desire to know God. Everywhere there is a sense of confusion and strain and struggle. Increasingly, people long for something which satisfies but seem unable to find it. Many have pursued pleasure and personal enrichment, but few have arrived at contentment. As the early church leader, St. Augustine once observed, there is a God-shaped hole inside each of us and, therefore, only God can fill that hole.

The radiant life that so many seek will not be found in the "Broadway lights" that are chased if God is left behind in Nashville. Naturally, God is not limited in location, not geographical location, anyway. God is present in both Nashville and New York. The great question for every person is whether God is welcomed in the human heart. What the songwriter discovers is, "I was wrong for thinking you were something I could ever do without." And at the end of the journey which pursues the radiant life, the song writer finally discovers what we all must discover, "You (God) were all that I needed all along." It is there, at the end, we realize that, just like a deer that craves streams of water, the life we crave is found in God.

Lord, when I have wandered away from you, help me once again to find my way back to your embrace. Amen.

No Place Available

"She gave birth to her firstborn child, a son, wrapped him snugly, and laid him in a manger, because there was no place for them in the guestroom."
Luke 2:7 (Common English Bible)

No single incident in Jesus' life captures more powerfully, and clearly, his reception here on earth: "there was no place for them." In only moments prior to his birth, the words were spoken, "no place." In his life, there would be no place in people's hearts for a meaningful relationship with him. During his ministry, there would be no place for his teachings in the minds of those who heard him. In the synagogue, there would be no place for his prophetic message. As Harry Emerson Fosdick once observed, "inhospitality was the central tragedy of Jesus' life."[22]

Today, this remains a difficulty for Jesus, finding a place in our lives. It has been suggested that atheism – the denial of God's existence – is not the major enemy of Christianity. The major enemy of the Christian faith is the inhospitality of those who will say that they believe in Jesus. Belief is important. It is the beginning place of a vital, life-giving faith. But belief without hospitality, belief without making a place for Jesus in one's life, results in the suffocation of faith. Faith is nourished and grows in strength by an ongoing, daily relationship with Jesus. Neglect any relationship, fail to make a place for those who love you, and the consequence is the loss of that relationship.

Some will say that the difficulty is simply overcrowded lives. We have become increasingly busy and there is little "place in our life" left over at the end of the day. Few will question how busy we have become. That would be difficult to debate. The question that presses is, "Busy doing what?" What occupies the place of those hours that we are awake? We find places for the things we really care about. We may say that there is no place for Jesus in our life today. And then we say the same thing tomorrow. We then discover that weeks have passed without any meaningful time with God and God's Word in the Bible. What is inescapable is that we gave our time to matters for which we cared more deeply than Jesus.

Tonight is Christmas Eve. What we recall tonight is the birth of the Christ child. Most people know that, believers and unbelievers. But there is something else that happens on this night, something that we would do well not to forget. For the first time, the words, "there is no place" is spoken. There is no place in the guestroom for the family of Jesus Christ; no place for Jesus to be born. Someone once wisely said, "You can't un-ring the bell." Well, there is nothing we can do about those words spoken so long ago, "there is no place." But tonight, as we remember and celebrate the birth of Jesus, we can answer for ourselves, "Will there be a place for Jesus in our life?"

It's almost here, the birthday of my Lord. Make my heart receptive to welcome him. Amen.

---

[22]Harry Emerson Fosdick, "Hospitality to the Highest", *Riverside Sermons* (New York: Harper & Brothers, 1958), 275.

If I Told You

"But God shows his love for us, because while we were still sinners Christ died for us."
Romans 5:8 (Common English Bible)

In his heartfelt country ballad, *If I Told You*, Darius Rucker asks someone to love him in spite of his faults and shortcomings. Written by Ross Copperman, Jon Nite and Shane McAnally, the song's lyrics are a plea for acceptance, for understanding, and for love, though he recognizes that it is not deserved. "What if I told you sometimes I lose my faith? I wonder why someone like you would even talk to me." Brokenness runs deep in the words as the song fleshes out a brief narrative of a life that is lived without a father. The visual that is sketched for the listener is quite vivid and one that many people will relate to. Every life is a mixture of brokenness and wholeness, regrets and fulfillments – each with varying degrees of one and the other. Yet, in the middle of it all is the desire of every person to be loved.

Perhaps no fear grips a life quite like the fear that one is unworthy of love. The apostle Paul knows this fear in his own life. Yet, because of Jesus Christ, Paul has richly discovered a love that puzzles, even defies comprehension: "But God shows his love for us, because while we were sinners Christ died for us." Love and acceptance is not negotiated. Love is not withheld until we clean-up the mess of our lives. God's love is freely given to each of us in the very midst of the wreckage of our lives. And it is there that we desire it the most, as Darius Rucker sings, "If I told you the mess that I can be. When there's no one there to see. Would you look the other way, cause you love me anyway?" The plea is urgent – in this song and in the depths of our own hearts.

A life not well lived, a life soiled by regrettable decisions and stupid things has an enormous weight that bears down upon our chest and denies life-giving breath into our lungs. Such a life, lived day by day, becomes increasingly sorrowful. Questions of self-worth well-up in the heart multiplying the pain of an already broken life. The plea of the song becomes our own, "If I told you all the stupid things I've done. I'd blamed on being young. But I was old enough to know, I know. If I told you the mess that I can be, when there's no one there to see. Could you look the other way cause you love me anyway? Cause you love me anyway." The song then ends with the plea becoming more poignant, "Could you love me anyway, *please?*"

Paul wants us to know that God loves us anyway: "while we were sinners Christ died for us." This makes all the difference in our lives. Sorrow and brokenness is replaced with joy and gratitude. A relationship with God – once broken by our poorly lived lives – is restored. The enormous weight that pressed against us is removed by an unseen hand and we draw rapidly a fresh breath into our lungs; a breath of hope for a new beginning. That is what God does for us. God nails our old, regrettable past upon the cross and gives us a fresh start. But now we begin with new knowledge – God's power and love abides with us, and will continue to do so even when we stumble again. That is because God loves us anyway.

I come to you, O God, as I am, with my sin and brokenness, knowing that your forgiving love is an everlasting promise. Amen.

The School of Christ

"Learn from me."
Matthew 11:29 (Common English Bible)

Building disciples of Jesus Christ – people, who voluntarily submit to the Lordship of Christ that results in the decision to learn from Christ, follow his example and participate in his ministry – is the will of God. This is God's ideal purpose. It is this purpose that believers attach themselves in baptism. The difficulty for some believers is that they haven't employed a helpful method to advance in the school of Christ. Their study is disorderly and usually results in failure. They rarely seem to rise above the rudiments of the spiritual journey and remain disillusioned by their lack of spiritual progress. Jesus' own life and ministry provides help; provides the secret of learning that, when applied to our discipleship to Christ, produces fruit in the striving toward spiritual maturity.

If, then, we would learn of Christ, we must begin with the words he spoke. The twelve disciples who followed Jesus throughout his three-year ministry heard his words spoken to them. Today, those who follow Christ have those spoken words recorded in the four Gospels of Matthew, Mark, Luke and John. So, we begin where the original twelve disciples began; we **Read** the words of Jesus. With the spirit of inquisitiveness, we read deeply the words of Jesus, alert to those qualities and values that shaped his character and revealed his laser-like focus on being useful to God. There is simply no substitute for reading Christ's words if we are to pass from stage to stage in the school of Christ.

Then let us pause sufficiently to **Reflect** on what we have read. Knowledge of Jesus' words without application is inadequate. The object here is to grasp the light of Christ's teaching and cast it before our footsteps. Christ's teaching to the disciples was always followed by a measure of explanation, challenging the disciples to apply the ideals and principals to immediate life. We don't ask nearly enough those of questions that move us from one step to another in our forward march in the school of Christ. Today we are helped by many fine devotionals and scholarly commentaries that probe deeply into the meaning and practical application of Jesus' words. Select a trusted devotional guide for processing the truth of Christ's teaching and its usefulness for our lives.

Respond! We shall never really know Christ, as he desires to be known, until we begin to respond to what we have grasped of his teaching. Until Christ's teaching becomes instruction for daily practice, our lives remain unchanged. We study a musical instrument so that we may enjoy the music that we bring from it. We study another language to enrich our knowledge, enjoyment and appreciation of another culture. A musical instrument never played, and another language never spoken has no effect upon our lives. Similarly, only in our obedient response to Jesus' teachings does the beauty of our Savior's instruction grow upon our lives. Read, Reflect and Respond. This is Jesus' method for advancing in The School of Christ.

May my heart be willingly ground in which you shape and nurture the new things you desire to bring about. In Christ's name I ask. Amen.

There's A Girl

"I was beaten with rods three times. I was stoned once. I was shipwrecked three times. I spent a day and a night on the open sea."
2 Corinthians 11:25 (Common English Bible)

Trent Harmon shared recently that his country single, *There's A Girl*, was inspired not by one girl, but by several romances that Harmon has experienced. With an upbeat and happy tempo, the song is about how guys are driven by girls and how they drive guys to do things they normally wouldn't do. "Why would we drive six hundred miles one way? Blow through cash that we ain't made. Get tattoos, wash our trucks, push and press our luck." The storytelling is crisp and true, a light-hearted look at the old, well-worn phrase, "love makes you do crazy things." The song is deeply heartfelt and romantic while also poking fun at himself for all the stupid things he does when a girl consumes his attention.

In his letter to the Corinthian Church, the apostle Paul is singing a similar song, "I was beaten with rods three times. I was stoned once. I was shipwrecked three times. I spent a day and a night on the open sea." Why would any rational person subject themselves to these things? They wouldn't. And that is precisely Paul's point. Trent Harmon does stupid things because, "There's A Girl," and Paul opens himself to such mistreatment and danger because, "There is a man named Jesus" who has overtaken any rational thought. Harmon has been taken captive by his love for a girl; Paul has been taken captive by Jesus' love for Paul. A lyric in Harmon's song is, "Why does any man do anything in the whole damn world?" The apostle Paul has an answer. It is love.

Paul acknowledges in his letter to the Corinthian Church that he is bragging when he shares all he has suffered. But Paul is equally clear that this bragging is not for self-aggrandizement. What Paul urgently wants the reader to hear is that there is a man, a man named Jesus, and that if you pay attention to that man, his love for you will get to you; his love for you will result in you doing stupid and irrational things. The love of Jesus Christ is so pervasive that neither beatings, or stoning, or being shipwrecked can drive that love out of you.

Naturally, what Paul desires by his "bragging" is that we would become curious about this kind of love. Trent Harmon sings, "Why would we ask when we know we can't dance? Show our hands and change our plans. Lose our minds, break our hearts and learn to play guitar. Why does any man do anything in the whole damn world? 'Cause there's a girl. 'Cause there's a girl." Why would Paul place himself in harm's way, suffer beatings and endure stoning and spend a night and day on an open sea when that is so dangerous? Because there's a man who has gotten to him. And Paul wants you to know him also.

I love you, O God, for you give me breath and life. May I so embody your love that your loving presence is unmistakable to everyone I meet today. Amen.

Sabal Palmetto

"After a whirlwind passes by, the wicked are no more, but the righteous stand firm forever."
Proverbs 10:25 (Common English Bible)

This official Florida state tree boasts a higher wind resistance than any other palm, according to a research study conducted by Mary Duryea, University of Florida associate dean of research, and reported in an issue of *Coastal Living* magazine.[23] Consequently, this is one of the trees most favored by landscapers when planting by the shore. Strong Caribbean winds have little effect upon the Sabal Palmetto. They remain, for the most part, unshakeable in all conditions of weather.

A major theme of Proverbs, and notably of this passage, is that how we choose to live has ultimate consequences. Those who live foolishly are those who have chosen to live according to every desire of their heart. This is a decision to ignore the wisdom of God and God's direction for living. When the storms of life blow, as they inevitably do for each of us, we are swept away. This is not God's punishment for ignoring God's wisdom. Becoming "swept away" by the strong winds that beat against us, from time to time, is the natural consequence of the poor decisions we make. It is no different from the natural consequence of choosing to plant a tree by the shore that has low wind tolerance.

A poor landscaping choice, when selecting a tree to plant near the shore, is the Washington Fan Palm. This tree scores low on wind-resistance. The selection of this tree to plant near the sea indicates that no care was given to the decision or that the conventional wisdom for landscaping was ignored. The inevitable result, during a tropical storm, is that this tree is likely to be uprooted and swept away. The landscaping will be, as Proverbs states it, "no more." It is simply a natural consequence of a poor landscaping decision.

Proverbs announces that God has rigged the universe for righteousness – that is, life that is built upon wisdom shall, "stand firm forever." God's ways are not simply a preference that God has for our lives. God understands what makes life work, and what makes life fail. God's wisdom, shared generously in the scriptures, is simply a gracious invitation to live wisely, that we may endure the storms that come in every life. And when the strong Caribbean winds of hardship and difficulty blow across our path, we will stand firm. That is because our life has been planted on the enduring foundation of God's wisdom.

Establish us in your wisdom, O Lord. Nurture us, day by day, in your word that never fails to point us to the way of life and strengthens us for the storms that are inevitable. In Christ's name, we ask. Amen.

---

[23]Marisa Spyker, "5 Trees to Plant by the Sea: What works (and what doesn't) when it comes to planting trees by the shore," *Coastal Living*, March 2013.

The Long Way

"God's riches, wisdom, and knowledge are so deep! They are as mysterious as his judgements, and they are as hard to track as his paths!"
Romans 11:33 (Common English Bible)

The Long Way is a midtempo country ballad written and recorded by American country music singer Brett Eldredge. Matthew Rogers co-wrote the song. Eldredge says that the song is "a look into what I want to find in love."[24] Careful attention to the lyrics reveals how someone can get to know their partner on a deeper level by paying attention to the particulars and nuances of their life; by learning deeply about their history and hometown. Eldredge says that he co-wrote the song with Rogers during a time when he was looking for true love. Matthew Rogers was engaged to be married during the writing and the circumstances of the two writers inspired the romantic lyrics.

Here, in his letter to the Christian Church in Rome, the Apostle Paul shares that he has taken *The Long Way* in his deep desire to know God: "God's riches, wisdom, and knowledge are so deep! They are as mysterious as his judgements, and they are as hard to track as his paths!" (Romans 11:33). Paul has sought "to track" God's paths, to explore deeply all he can discover about God. Paul longs to bathe in as much detail of God's backstory as possible; God's riches, God's wisdom, God's knowledge, and God's judgements. Paul wants it all. Paul has come to a deeper knowledge of God in the person of Jesus Christ and that knowledge – and personal experience of Jesus on the road to Damascus – has changed him. Paul dearly loves and constantly delights in his "heavenly Father" made real to earth in Jesus.

The Long Way is a song that I wish I had written. I have downloaded the song and listen to it during my morning runs. "Take me the long way around your town. Were you the queen with the silver crown? I want the secrets you keep, the shine underneath. Of the diamond I think I just found. Take me the long way around." As I approach the thirty-first anniversary of marriage to my wife, Grace, I can't seem to discover enough about her. Grace is a diamond that I was fortunate enough to stumble upon so many years ago and my love for her seems to grow more expansive each day. Gladly, I take *The Long Way* in searching for the riches that makes her the woman she is. I don't want to miss anything.

Paul doesn't want to miss anything about his Lord. In a world where we don't have meaningful conversations anymore with those we love, distracted by this and that, Paul invites us to slow down. Put away the mobile phones and the iPads and social media platforms and listen to God in the Holy Scriptures, The Bible. Permit your mind – and heart – to take *The Long Way* to discover again this great and beautiful God we see in Jesus Christ. Once we have, our hearts will sing along with Brett Eldredge, "Didn't think tonight when I walked in, I'd be falling for somewhere I've never been."

My life is filled with obligations and commitments, but none are greater than knowing you. In my daily moments of quiet, open my heart to know you more fully. Amen.

---

[24] Kelly Brickey, "Brett Eldredge Gets Vulnerable About Love in 'The Long Way.'" *(Sounds Like Nashville:* SpinMedia, August 11, 2017).

What God Does for Us
(Location: Via Dolorosa)

"When Pilate heard these words, he led Jesus out and seated him on the judge's bench at the place called Stone Pavement. It was about noon on the Preparation Day for the Passover. Pilate said to the Jewish leaders, 'Here's your king.'"
John 19:13, 14 (Common English Bible)

Via Dolorosa means the way of grief. Historians and archaeologists disagree over the precise route that awful procession would have taken; the route Jesus took to the cross. What is certain is that it would become a route marked with grief. But the route to the cross began from a place known as the Stone Pavement, part of the Tower of Antonia bordering the northwest corner of the Temple complex. It is here that Jesus is tried before Pilate. It is here that Jesus is sentenced to flogging and crucifixion.

Jesus walked the Via Dolorosa alone. The twelve men who shared in Jesus' ministry, the twelve who shared a meal with Jesus only the night before are not with him. What is likely is that they are hiding behind a locked door, questioning the abrupt arrest of Jesus and what that now meant for them. Specifics of their location are unavailable – only that they are not with Jesus. Perhaps they are experiencing shame, horror and disbelief. Their golden dream has now turned into a nightmare.

Tom Wright, that wonderful teacher of our faith, says that the absence of the disciples is important. Jesus had to walk the Via Dolorosa alone. It is a major problem in Christian devotion, suggests Wright, that when we think of the way of the cross we so often think of Jesus as the great example, with ourselves simply imitating him.[25] Actually, central to our faith is the conviction that Jesus must do for us what we cannot. An important point of the Via Dolorosa is that Jesus must walk it alone.

Jesus suffers so that others need not; Jesus dies so that others may not. Pilgrims who walk the Via Dolorosa today do so for many reasons. Some make the journey out of simple curiosity. Others wish to shop the endless souvenirs that are sold along the route. All jostle in the narrow streets and alleyways. But perhaps an authentic walk along the Via Dolorosa is one where we realize that here Jesus walked on our behalf, that this way of grief was an achievement, an accomplishment that could only be completed by God's Son. This is a walk best completed in silence and reverence.

Grant, this day, O God, a renewed sense of awe and reverence for what you accomplished for me in the way of the cross, the journey of grief. Amen.

---

[25] Tom Wright, *The Way of the Lord: Christian Pilgrimage Today* (Grand Rapids, MI: Eerdmans Publishing Company, 1999), 95.

Better Man

"I don't do the good that I want to do, but I do the evil that I don't want to do."
Romans 7:19 (Common English Bible)

Country artist, Taylor Swift, may have written the saddest song I have ever heard, *Better Man*, performed by Little Big Town. There is considerable speculation as to which one of her former boyfriends occupied her thoughts as she wrote the lyrics – the song speaking clearly to a breakup. Rich, and often times vulnerable, emotions push the story arch forward of a man who failed to return his best for the love and devotion he received, "And I gave you my best and we both know you can't say that, you can't say that. I wish you were a better man." The chorus opens a window to a broken heart, "Sometimes, in the middle of the night, I can feel you again," Little Big Town sings. "But I just miss you, and I just wish you were a better man."

Listen carefully to the apostle Paul, here in the seventh chapter of his letter to the Roman Church, and you can almost hear him humming these telling lyrics. The exception – and this is important – Paul isn't grieving over a difficult romantic breakup. Paul's grief is that he wants desperately to be that better man, "I don't do the good that I want to do, but I do the evil that I don't want to do." The deep emotion captured in the song, *Better Man*, is fully present in Paul's words. Paul has experienced a deep love from his lord, Jesus Christ, and has no desire to remain the man he was. Paul desires deeply to be a better man because of Jesus.

Paul is overwhelmed by the magnitude of God's love for him in the person of Jesus. That love has made Paul fully alert to his own failure to love God – and others – with equal scale. Self-examination reveals a man driven by selfish desire and harmful thoughts and behaviors directed to those he disagrees with. Indeed, Paul confesses to having others beaten and put to death simply because he did not share their faith convictions. Yet, God shows-up in a vision, addresses Paul as he travels to Damascus to inflict more harm on others, and loves him. It is a love that breaks Paul; a love that drives Paul not only to repentance, but a love that results in an intense wish to be something more. It is a love that drives Paul to be a better man.

The absence of a vision, the intention and location of a means to become more as a follower of Jesus Christ may boil down to one thing: the failure to experience deeply and richly the depth of God's love demonstrated for us in the crucifixion, death and resurrection of Jesus Christ. Any plan to nurture personal faith will fail unless time is given first to reflect profoundly and constantly on God's love such that we experience delight in God. The result of noticing God in this manner will be an increasing desire to be a better person. This must then be followed by intentional practices that remove our automatic rebellion to God's purposes for our lives. It is here, noticing God afresh and practicing disciplines for spiritual growth that Paul becomes that better man. The same will be true for us.

Following you is never easy, O God. Often it is exhausting, sometimes discouraging. Open my heart to your presence every moment and direct my steps that I may walk closely with you. Amen.

About the Author

Dr. Hood, the pastor of the First Presbyterian Church of Delray Beach, learned from his friend and mentor, Bryant Kirkland, that effective preaching and writing demands careful listening – listening to the conversations of ordinary people in the community where he pastors. Such conversations reveal the problems and concerns that are uppermost in the minds of the people. In these brief meditations, Dr. Hood addresses what he has heard with compassion, insight and directness. Most importantly, he refrains from offering personal opinions. Always, he invites the reader to listen to God's Word and the light it shines on the struggles of the present day.

www.ingramcontent.com/pod-product-compliance
Lightning Source LLC
Chambersburg PA
CBHW071306110526
44591CB00010B/801